The Field Guide to Rapid Process Improvement Workshops in Healthcare

This book takes the reader through the process to plan, deliver, and follow-up a weeklong Lean Quality Improvement event, usually termed a 'Rapid Improvement Event' or 'Rapid Process Improvement Workshop (RPIW).' Drawing on the experience of conducting over 100 of these workshops, the book gives readers the information to plan and run their own event. It describes how RPIWs fit in to wider improvement processes and how the reader can maximize these processes in their own organization

These weeklong improvement events are popular in health and social care, but there are no textbooks available to support them. There are several books that describe the use of shorter Kaizen events in health care, but none that describe the process of delivering weeklong events. The events have a rhythm specific to the one-week format, and the book seeks to help people to make use of best practice and to avoid common problems.

Based on the experiences of the authors, this book includes an introduction to Lean concepts linked to the relevant part of the process description; examples and templates of forms that can be used in workshops; and photographs of actual events.

The Field Guide to Rapid Process Improvement Workshops in Healthcare

Applying Lean to Improve Quality and Patient Experience

Cameron Stark, Gavin Hookway, Gill McVicar and Hugo van Woerden

Routledge
Taylor & Francis Group

A PRODUCTIVITY PRESS BOOK

First published 2024
by Routledge
605 Third Avenue, New York, NY 10158

and by Routledge
4 Park Square, Milton Park, Abingdon, Oxon, OX14 4RN

Routledge is an imprint of the Taylor & Francis Group, an informa business

ISBN: 978-0-367-07439-5 (hbk)
ISBN: 978-0-367-07435-7 (pbk)
ISBN: 978-0-429-02074-2 (ebk)

DOI: 10.4324/9780429020742

Typeset in Garamond
by Deanta Global Publishing Services, Chennai, India

Gavin Hookway: To the memory of my friend and colleague Murdina Campbell

Gill McVicar: For my family.

Contents

Acknowledgements

Gavin Hookway gratefully acknowledges training, coaching and support for the RPIWs he undertook from Keith Appleby, Steven Bartley and Maureen Raine from the Tees, Esk and Wear Valley NHS Foundation Trust, Gill McVicar, Cameron Stark, Laurie Johnson, Rachel Buchanan, Gill Ford, Nicola Fraser, Derek Leslie, Jane Howe, Christina West, Lisa Kenley, Mairi Fraser, Mandy Leslie, Colin Farman and my wife Helen.

Cameron Stark thanks Diane Miller and Celeste Derheimer of the Virginia Mason Institute; Maureen Raine, Keith Appleby and Steven Bartley from Tees, Esk and Wear Valley NHS Foundation Trust in England; and Iain Smith, Associate Researcher at the Newcastle University Business School for training, coaching and support. He thanks Dr Adrian Baker, Dr Michelle Beatie, Murdina Campbell, Kay Cordiner, Pam Cremin, Dr Paul Davidson, Chrishan Folan, Gill Ford, Anne Gent, Gavin Hookway, Dr Jacqui Howes, Nick Kenton, Linda Kirkland, Rachel Mann, Elaine Mead, Sue Menzies, Cora MacLeod, Christian Nicolson, David Park, Neil Pellow, Rob Polson, Mr Andrew Pyott, Jocelyn Reid, Liz Smart and Neil Stewart for their support during RPIWs. Paul Arbuckle, Andy Crawford, Lesley-Anne Smith, Ruth Glassborrow and Dr. Emma Watson provided advice and encouragement in NHS Highland and the wider Scottish health system.

About the Authors

Cameron Stark, MB ChB, MPH, MSc (Dist), MRCPsych, FFPH, is an Honorary Reader and Part-time Lecturer at the University of the Highlands and Islands (UHI), Scotland. Cameron leads the UHI postgraduate module on the application of Lean in healthcare. After graduating from the University of Glasgow, UK, he trained in psychiatry and public health and worked as an NHS Public Health Doctor for over 30 years. Cameron was the Quality Improvement Science Lead for NHS Highland and trained as a Lean leader with Tees, Esk and Wear Valley NHS Foundation Trust. He has published over 60 papers in peer-reviewed journals, written 11 book chapters and written or edited 7 previous textbooks.

Gavin Hookway has over 30 years of experience working in healthcare within NHS Scotland, NHS England and Private/Independent Sectors. He has extensive knowledge of Operating Theatres, from both operational and managerial perspectives, and is driven to provide safe, high-quality patient care in the most efficient and equitable manner. Gavin is a certified Continuous Improvement Leader and Coach accredited through the Tees, Esk and Wear Valley NHS Foundation Trust. In 2022, Gavin founded Hookway Quality Improvement Services (HQIS), an online company which aims to support people and organisations through their improvement journey.

Gill McVicar originally trained as a nurse and midwife, working in several roles, latterly in the community in Highland. She left clinical practice to work as Quality Facilitator and then held many managerial posts within the NHS. She gained experience as Director of Operations and then, due to her passion for improving care and development of staff, moved back to focus on continuous quality improvement as Director of Quality and Transformation. After retiring from the NHS, Gill has worked as a Client Facilitation Consultant on developing a People Plan and supporting training and coaching in quality improvement and Lean methodologies. As well as clinical and professional qualifications, Gill has trained in Health Economics, and as a certified Lean Leader and Coach with the Virginia Mason Institute.

Hugo van Woerden is the Director of InsightPro Ltd, a small health consultancy. He is also Visiting Professor at the University of the Highlands and Islands, Scotland.

Copies of Materials Used in the Book

Copies of the blank forms used in the book are available from Hookway Quality Improvement Services (HQIS) using the QR code below.

https://www.hookwayqis.com

Chapter 1

Structure of the Book

Introduction

Rapid Process Improvement Workshops (RPIWs) are an important method for the application of Lean Production tools. Used in many industries, the use of RPIWs in healthcare has increased and they are often seen as a gold standard approach for applying Lean methods and delivering service improvements.

As this book discusses, RPIWs are not the only way of applying Lean methods to a problem, and other options may be preferable depending on the situation. Continuous improvement methods, smaller improvement events, value management and 3P (Production, Preparation, Process) events all have important roles to play. There is value in making improvements in any area, but it can be challenging to maintain gains when undertaking events without also introducing other aspects of Lean. Organisations differ in their readiness to implement Lean at scale, and good links between staff groups and between staff and management make widespread improvements more likely (Jones, 2022).

An evaluation of the application of Lean and the use of RPIWs in the English National Health Service concluded that the research,

> supports the role of RPIWs in providing timely solutions to the flow, quality of care, and environmental safety of patients and staff within specified value streams. As well as delivering 'rapid improvement', or 'quick wins', RPIWs provide an important opportunity for cross-functional collaboration, boosting staff morale and fostering employee empowerment.
>
> **(Burgess et al., 2022, p. 59)**

This book introduces the use of RPIWs in Lean practice. The form of an RPIW used in services varies and this volume gives an overview of a generic approach to RPIWs. Readers will want to adapt the approach to their own situation. The general format will also be helpful for people undertaking shorter improvement events. A case study of improvement work in an outpatient service is used to illustrate concepts. The approach is equally applicable to non-patient processes.

Chapter 2 provides a brief overview of Lean for readers who are new to the topic. If Lean is completely new, then it will be helpful to read this book in conjunction with our overview of the application of Lean in healthcare (Stark & Hookway, 2019), or one of the introductory Lean textbooks provided by other authors. Suggestions for further reading are provided in Chapter 2.

The chapter outlines the role of continuous improvement and the importance of clear aims, the use of Plan-Do-Study-Act (PDSA) cycles, and observation and measurement. The chapter also discusses the importance of engaging staff in improvement work and of respecting their role and that of service users. Organisational context is also important, particularly the stage of application of Lean that has been reached by an organisation (Mead et al., 2023).

Chapter 3 discusses the first steps of an RPIW. RPIWs are expensive events that consume a great deal of time and energy. Careful appraisal of the need for an event is essential. This chapter reviews other possible responses including continuous improvement and shorter two- or three-day events. Understanding the problem and the context is necessary, and the chapter reviews the type of information that is required for a decision.

Clarity of purpose and clear aims are important, as is identifying the nature of the problem. Pre-existing

DOI: 10.4324/9780429020742-1

disputes over conditions or animosity between members of a team will rarely be resolved by an RPIW. Some matters are better settled by other mechanisms. When an RPIW is a good option, information gathering in advance of a first meeting to scope the nature of the problem is helpful. An organisational Sponsor must be present at this meeting, as well as the person in charge of the area of work being reviewed (termed the Process Owner in this volume). At least one and preferably two facilitators to support the work are needed.

Chapter 4 reviews the work that is needed in advance of an event. The event described is based on a five-day workshop, running from Monday to Friday. For shorter events, readers should make appropriate adjustments.

Observations and data gathering are essential, and the chapter describes the type of information that is likely to be necessary. It gives information on the identification of Lead Time and Cycle Time and calculation of 'takt time'. The chapter describes the use of key documents to help the work. Useful documents include Direct Observation Record, Process Work Sheets and Work Combination Records.

Involving the team is very important. There are two groups in an RPIW: the Home Team who work in the service as normal during the RPIW week, and the Away Team who are freed from their other duties for the week. Methods of promoting team involvement include briefings and the opportunity to offer ideas and views on the processes. The chapter recommends the use of Waste Wheels and Ideas Forms to gather information and promote engagement.

Chapter 5 expands on team and engagement and discusses how to conduct a Process Mapping exercise with a team. The value of representing all disciplines and grades is noted, and practice tips are offered for use when conducting the exercise. Setting the tone of an RPIW is needed at all stages, and the conduct of the mapping exercise must reflect respect for staff and demonstrate that their views are valued and wanted.

Chapter 6 identifies the meetings that are needed in preparation for the event and suggests what should be covered at each meeting. Time needs to be set aside for work between meetings, and senior attendance from the Sponsor is essential in demonstrating organisational commitment. A reasonable approach is to have four planning meetings over four to six weeks. The focus of the meetings gradually shifts from collection of information to finalising targets and ensuring preparation for the event is complete and that the conditions are right for the maximum benefit possible from the RPIWs. The value of involving staff in neighbouring services, and in services which may learn from the event is noted. Approaches to patient involvement are discussed.

Chapter 7 covers the work the day before the RPIW, or the working day before if the event is to commence on a Monday. The room the event is to be conducted in has to be prepared and the correct materials present to allow the event to flow as well as possible.

Chapter 8 reviews Day One of the event. Some of the team members will be anxious and offering support and setting the tone of the RPIW is a good first step. Patient representatives are likely to benefit from support by the facilitators. The Sponsor can help with this by attending the first session, setting the context and challenging the team to make the most of the event. Teaching of relevant methods will usually be required, and possible topics are suggested. Data collected should be reviewed and methods of walking the team through the data are discussed. Capturing team ideas is always important and the chapter suggests actions such as frequent use of Ideas Forms and adding to the Waste Wheels as new wastes are identified by the team.

Chapter 9 reviews the conduct of Day Two, including the development of an Ideal Future State map. Matching 'ideas' and 'wastes' and identifying workstreams are important. The conduct of workstreams is described, including the need to move people between workstreams when their skills are required in other workstreams. A key focus of Day Two is moving people from contemplation to action, and the commencement of measured Plan-Do-Study-Act (PDSA) cycles. Some members of the team may be anxious about their ability to contribute, particularly if they are in junior positions, and ways of supporting them are suggested.

Chapter 10 discusses Days Three and Four. These are the engine rooms of the event where most testing is undertaken. It is important for the facilitators and Process Owners to maintain momentum and to keep track of progress on workstreams, including closing down workstreams and opening new workstreams as progress is made. Keeping the Away Team involved reaps benefits both from the learning within the RPIW and for ensuring progress after the event. Documentation to record the impact is important and good use of PDSA cycles is required.

Chapter 11 reviews preparation for a final presentation of the work undertaken during the week. It suggests a structure for presentations and notes the value of inclusion of the Home Team either in the presentation or as a separate event in the workplace.

Chapter 12 discusses the work needed after an RPIW to maintain momentum. The work of the Process Owner is very important, and continued measurement, and further change, is the best approach.

Chapter 13 presents the management context of an RPIW and adds to the argument that building in Daily Management and a wider organisational Lean

Management System will bring the greatest long-term changes. This will not be the situation in many organisations, and ways of continuing change in less supported contexts are discussed.

Chapter 14 summarises the work in the book and suggests further reading.

Illustrations used in this volume include forms supplied by Hookway Quality Improvement Services (HQIS), run by book co-author Gavin Hookway. A QR code to allow the download of PDF copies of the forms from the HQIS website is included on page xvii.

Conclusion

RPIWs are not the only way of supporting change, but they are a useful method in the right situation and can engage staff at scale. This book presents an approach to running an RPIW that can also be adapted to shorter events.

References

Burgess, N., Currie, G., Crump, B., & Dawson, A. (2022). *Leading change across a healthcare system: How to build improvement capability and foster a culture of continuous improvement, Report of the Evaluation of the NHS-VMI partnership.* Warwick Business School. https://warwick.ac.uk/fac/soc/wbs/research/vmi-nhs/reports/report_-_leading_change_across_a_healthcare_system_22.09.2022.pdf

Jones, B. (2022). *Building an organisational culture of continuous improvement: Learning from the evaluation of the NHS partnership with Virginia Mason Institute.* Health Foundation. http://www.health.org.uk/publications/long-reads/building-an-organisational-culture-of-continuous-improvement

Mead, E., Stark, C., & Thomson, M. (2023). *International examples of lean in healthcare: Case studies of best practices.* Routledge.

Stark, C., & Hookway, G. (2019). *Applying lean in health and social care services.* Routledge.

Chapter 2

Lean in Health and Social Care Services

Introduction

Improving quality in health and social care services is a planet-wide aim. Funding models for services vary including insurance-based systems, co-payment arrangements, private purchase and state funding. Whatever the financial arrangements, people expect the best quality of care possible within the financial constraints of the service.

Delivering value to service users requires providers to identify what users need and want; make processes as efficient as possible, while being responsive to individual needs and preferences; minimise errors and reduce as far as possible the likelihood that errors in care lead to harm to service users; and keep wait times down, while also controlling costs.

Pressures in both health and social care have increased across the world. Low- and middle-income countries often have young and expanding populations whose care needs must be balanced against the ability of the nation to pay for care in whichever way it sees fit. More affluent countries often have ageing populations and access to new, expensive treatments which also demands an ongoing focus on effectiveness and efficiency.

In the UK, an ageing population brings large social care costs. Healthcare services, built around a model of primary care services, and specialist secondary care services based in outpatient clinics and hospitals, struggle to support people with multiple health conditions and who are frail. The links between primary and secondary care have become ever more important, as older people move back and forwards between community care, hospital care and sometimes residential care. Breakdowns in any part of these complex processes can lead to people being stranded in inappropriate settings that do not best meet their needs.

An increase in the number of people with dementia, linked to longer life expectancy and therefore increased likelihood of developing the condition, provides further strain on services. Expectations of access to good mental health services have also increased, as people become more willing to talk about mental health and to seek and expect an excellent quality of care.

New treatments bring great potential, but also potentially enormous costs. Insulin pumps controlled by smartphone; imaging of the bowel conducted by swallowing a capsule with a miniaturised camera; smart houses that monitor mobility and activity in older people who live alone and who choose to use the system – all these developments offer unprecedented opportunities to deliver care well. In the long term, some costs will balance out: controlling diabetes better reduces complications, many of which can be life-threatening or disabling for example.

Other costs are entirely new, particularly in healthcare. For example, routine genetic testing of some cancer types, biological treatments for arthritis, immunotherapy for cancer and individually tailored treatments built around a person's genetic profile can all bring great benefits for individuals, but the costs are huge. Developments in epigenetics and related fields suggest further new costs that are unlikely to be manageable within existing budgets. These developments also offer the risk for widening of the gap in available healthcare between affluent and less affluent countries.

While the precise nature of the pressures varies by country and funding system, challenges to service quality

DOI: 10.4324/9780429020742-2

exist in all services and all nations. This book discusses one route for targeting improvements at scale in health and social care services, with a focus on delivering the best quality care possible within the cost constraints of the service and funding model.

Quality Improvement Methods

There are many approaches to quality improvement. There is no clear academic evidence that one method is markedly better than another. Case studies and system comparisons suggest, however, that organisations that manage to improve quality tend to have features in common. These include:

- Senior support for quality improvement work
- Consistent use of methods over time
- Wide involvement of staff in improvement work
- Availability of specialist support and coaching
- Good training arrangements, to support staff to apply the agreed methods
- Quality improvement that links to management structures
- Effort to maintain gains and to spread learning in a systematic manner

There are advantages to using methods that are well tested. The precise blend of quality improvement methods that an organisation uses will vary, but keeping these criteria in mind is helpful in identifying conditions that, if maximised, are likely to support success.

Lean

Background

Lean is one of the best-known approaches to embedding quality in a system. The term 'Lean' is used to describe an approach to management and quality closely associated with Toyota. Toyota, and other Japanese companies, took teaching from W. Edwards Deming and other theorists and developed their own methods of managing quality at scale. The system was popularised in the West in the 1990s and introduced into manufacturing industries. The methods have gradually spread into health and social care. Well-known early examples of the use of Lean in healthcare in the US include the Virginia Mason Medical Center in Seattle, ThedaCare in Wisconsin, and organisations such as Intermountain in Utah, Cincinnati Children's Hospital, Bellin Health in Michigan and the US Department of Veterans Affairs.

In Europe, Bolton in the UK and a group of NHS Trusts in North East England were early adopters. Elsewhere in Europe, services in Barcelona, Spain, the Netherlands and Italy applied Lean to healthcare. NHS Highland was the first Scottish health and social care organisation to use Lean at scale.

Lean as an Approach to Quality

Lean has three key aspects – a set of values, improvement methods and a management system. This volume deals with one type of application of Lean, in set-piece improvement workshops. It emphasises methods and values. It is important to keep in mind that Lean principles can be applied in other ways, and that Rapid Process Improvement Workshops (RPIWs) are not the only way – and not always the best way, depending on the circumstances – of applying Lean in health and social care. RPIWs allow many linked Plan-Do-Study-Act (PDSA) cycles to be conducted quickly, but this is not always required. Identifying which situations are most appropriate for RPIWs or other types of approaches is discussed in Chapter 3.

Lean methods are dealt with in detail in our previous book *Applying Lean in Health and Social Care* (Stark & Hookway, 2019) and in books by other authors. Suggested further reading is included at the end of this chapter. It is helpful to give a brief overview of Lean at this point to allow new readers to put the methods discussed in this book in context. Readers who are already well versed in Lean may prefer to go direct to the description of the stages of an RPIW.

Principles

The underpinning values of Lean are an assumption that the people who have the greatest insight into a problem are the people who, in the case of health and social care, provide that service and the people who use that service. It assumes that staff are motivated to deliver the best service they can to their clients or patients and that, if given the opportunity, they will be able to improve the processes they use to increase value, decrease waste and improve safety.

Lean, then, requires respect for staff and a focus on supporting front-line staff to make changes to the services that they deliver. There is also an implicit assumption that staff will want to take part in improvement activities. Our collective experience in over 100 RPIWs is that the great majority of staff become energised and engaged once they see evidence that their experience and expertise are acknowledged, and that their knowledge is core to the improvement work to be undertaken.

Value and Waste

Lean focuses on identifying value from the point of view of the customer – in the case of healthcare that is the client or patient – and aligning processes to increase delivery of any missing value that is identified. In Lean usage, for an activity to be of value, it must:

- Get the patient or service user closer to their goal, whatever it may be for that particular service
- Transform the product or service in some way
- Be done right the first time

If an activity is a support function, such as a Human Resources team, Finance or Estates, then there should still be a clear association between the processes used and the benefit to the user of the services. For example, a Human Resources team can improve services by making the recruitment process quick and effective and by helping the organisation to recruit the most appropriate staff. Similar considerations apply to Finance and Estates examples, and other back-room services which may not be visible to the person using the service but must function well to allow the service to be delivered.

The second point, transforming the service in some way, is easy to overlook, but is core to ideas of value and waste in Lean practice. Many activities add value to the person using the service: an assessment of their condition or problem will usually be essential for example and, if done well, has obvious value. Asking questions which are not then used in deciding treatment, but which are included to complete a form that may not be relevant to the person's issue, does not add any value and, in Lean, is therefore waste. This type of waste is termed 'absolute waste', and the aim is to remove it completely when it is identified.

Typing the same details of the assessment into two electronic systems because they do not communicate with one another, but the information is needed in both systems, also does not add value, as there is no transformation that enhances the product or service. It is an action which is necessary because of a current problem with a system. This type of waste can be thought of as a Necessary Non-Value-Added Activity: it is something you have to do at present, but the team should do its best to reduce it, and should review it periodically to see if it is still necessary, or if a new method of avoiding it can be identified.

An action, however appropriate, which is performed incorrectly, does not add value for the person using the service. If the error is not identified, it may result in a defect in care, with potential harm to the service user. If the error is identified, there will usually be further work to correct it – often termed 'rework'. This is an activity which would not have occurred if the original action had been correct. Health and social care organisations often have teams whose sole task is to identify, investigate and apologise for errors. This entails significant effort and staff time. It does not add value and can be markedly reduced by improving processes to avoid errors occurring in the future.

BOX 2.1   ACTIVITY – VALUE AND WASTE

For your service, what is the value that you provide to clients or patients? Which of your processes add this value, and which are examples of waste?

Types of Waste

It is useful to distinguish between types of waste. There are eight commonly used categories:

Waiting: People waiting for a service to be provided or staff waiting for patients, supplies or equipment.

Overprocessing: Unnecessary steps that add no value from the patient or service user's perspective.

Defects: Work that contains errors, and the effort of correcting the errors (sometimes termed 'rework').

Transportation: The movement of equipment or materials when this does not add value.

Motion: The movement of patients or staff.

Overproduction: Producing more than is needed, or faster than is needed.

Inventory: Having more stock than is needed.

Talent: Not making best use of the talent and experience available in a team.

Other categories of waste used by some organisations include unused wasted energy, water and natural resources (Stark & Hookway, 2019, pp. 18–28).

Continuous Flow

People working in health and social care services are usually busy people. Their working day involves constant activity, and even taking a scheduled break may be difficult. For the person experiencing a service, however, the experience will often be full of starts and stops.

Consider a frail older person who has a fall at home. If a fracture or other injury is suspected, they may have to travel to the hospital in an ambulance. There will often be a wait in the Emergency Department (ED) to be assessed. If tests such as an X-ray are ordered, there may be a delay before the X-ray takes place. There can then be a further delay before the X-ray is interpreted by a clinician, and a decision is made. If no injury has occurred that requires hospital treatment, there will often be another delay while transport is arranged to take the person home.

The ED may recommend or refer the person directly to a community service which assesses the risk of future falls and offers interventions. Typically, there will be a delay while the hospital communicates with that service or with the person's General Practitioner, and then more time will pass before the service contact the person and arrange to come to see the client. Once the person is assessed at home, they may wait for a place in a group that offers falls prevention activities, such as balance and strength training exercises. If they need adaptations to their home, like guard rails, ramps or a stair lift, they will often wait while this is organised and fitted.

For the staff working in the service, the activity is constant. For the person using the service, there are frequent delays. At times, they may wonder if anything is happening at all as the process is largely invisible to them, other than at touch points where they have contact with the services. There may be no way of them knowing where they are in a queue, or sometimes even of being sure that they are in a queue at all, sometimes resulting in phone calls to check, and even re-referral to the service because of delays.

This is an example of a push system, where each step of the process pushes the person on to the next part of the system, whether or not there is capacity. Queues develop at different parts of the system. By and large, no one delivering the services will know exactly who is waiting for what service in total, particularly if there are queues for different services in different areas. The person undertaking an assessment for a falls prevention service may know when the next group is scheduled, but they may not know if there is space in the next group, or if the person referred will have to wait. The staff ordering adaptations to the older person's home may not be aware of the schedules of the people who fit the adaptations, or even if the aid required is in stock at present or will have to be ordered.

Lean tries, as far as possible, to produce a continuous flow where people move seamlessly from one part of the required process to the next. Work in RPIWs often has a significant component of work on flow.

BOX 2.2   ACTIVITY – FLOW IN YOUR SERVICE

Consider your own services. Are there areas where is flow disrupted? Are there examples of push systems? What are the causes of the flow problems?

Levelling

Balancing capacity and demand is important. When there is more capacity than demand, staff wait for clients or patients, and when there is more demand than capacity, clients wait to be seen, although not all queues are caused by capacity problems. There are good reasons for not expecting health and social care services to work at full capacity all the time but having capacity and demand as balanced as possible is a useful principle to consider.

When services are elective, such as outpatient services or elective surgery, options for 'levelling' are easier to see, as they can control the rate at which people are offered procedures or appointments and can balance capacity across a working week and year.

Where services respond to emergencies and urgent requests, such as Child Protection alerts, or someone who has collapsed, there is very little opportunity to control the flow into the service. It is possible, however, to flex service provision in line with demand, at least to an extent. Individual emergencies are unpredictable, but emergency activity in aggregate is more predictable. In the Highlands of Scotland for example, EDs are busy even in the summer months when there are more outdoor activities, children are on holiday, and there are UK and overseas visitors to the area. Another example is that in many UK hospitals, most acute medical admissions occur between 10 am and 9 pm, with lower activity between 9 pm and 1 am, and then less admissions overnight. Admissions are higher on weekdays than at weekends, as people may put off contacting an emergency doctor until their General Practice opens on a Monday morning. Consequently, people admitted as emergencies at weekends are, on average, more ill than people admitted during the week. Children's psychology services are often quieter in the summer, as many children are referred by schools, and because children may feel under less pressure during the summer.

These are not absolute rules, of course, but it does mean there are patterns in local demand to which services can adapt. Services can also identify times when they have high volume activity, and the nature of the resource required to cope with it. The exact time of high demand will be unpredictable, but the existence of times of very high demand is predictable, and services can plan for how they will move resources to help in these times of high demand.

The concept of 'takt time' is useful in thinking about flow. Takt time is the pace at which a service must work to keep up with demand. It is calculated by dividing the time that the service is open for business by the number of, for example, new referrals that need to be seen. If a service is open for 36 hours a week and receives 72 referrals a week, then the takt time is 30 minutes (36 hours/72). This does not mean that only 30 minutes is available for each client, as there may be many staff in the service. It does, however, provide the service with a measure of whether they are keeping up with demand. If, at the end of a week, only 65 new clients have been seen, then the service is falling behind, and will begin to develop a queue. Knowing this gives some measure of real-time understanding of service flow. An example of a form that can be used to help calculate takt time is shown in Figure 2.1.

Multi-Process Operations and Multi-Skilled Workers

One way of responding to changes in demand is by thinking about multi-process operations and multi-skilled workers. Many health and social care services have multiple processes within them. These can be large-scale processes, such as appointment scheduling, clinic processes, investigations and so on, or smaller processes within a service. Many clinic appointments involve several assessments in the same clinic. For example, an audiology appointment may have a reception process, a hearing test, an assessment by a clinician and a session with a support worker who provides further information and contacts. For other people attending the same clinics, there may be processes that remove ear wax or fix hearing aids.

If one staff member does one process, it is difficult to flex up or down. The person is either 'at work' or not, and if they get behind there is often no one to help them. If each process is done by a separate person, and no one else knows how to undertake that process, then it is impossible to help them and, if they are absent for some reason, it may be very difficult or impossible to deliver that part of the work, with ensuing delays and recalls for further appointments.

If, however, services know what their individual processes are, and train people to be able to undertake more than one of these processes, then it becomes possible to move staff flexibly in response to changing pressures in the service. This also requires the service to know who is sufficiently skilled to deliver each process. A form called a 'Skills Matrix' can be used to keep track of this. An example is shown in Figure 2.2 Skills definitions are created by the service.

Multi-skilled workers are a familiar concept to most people from their experience in supermarkets. If queues exceed an agreed level, supermarkets in the UK will often call the staff from other activities to open a new till and work on it until the queues clear. In this example, the supermarkets will have determined the skills and competence required to undertake the activity, and they can return the person to their previous task once the increased activity is dealt with. Levelling and multi-process operations and multi-skilled workers are therefore closely related concepts.

People may have these skills but not have been able to use them for some time or may lack the confidence to do so. This is a waste of talent, and the use of the skills matrix and the conversations needed to complete it can help to identify the possession of the relevant skills. Where required support to refresh skills can be offered built into Personal Development Plans if required. This helps to release the relevant skills for the benefit of the team, organisation and patient who ultimately benefits.

Set-Up Reduction

Time spent preparing for a new process is termed 'set-up'. Time clearing things away after a procedure or process is often called 'tear down' time. In healthcare, operating theatres give an example of set-up and tear down time. Once a surgical team is ready for a new patient, the new patient will be brought from a waiting area or sometimes from a ward. They may walk, or they may be moved on a trolley depending on their condition and on the procedures used in the clinic or hospital. The person's identity will be confirmed, and they will be anaesthetised using the method appropriate for the operation. The procedure is conducted, the anaesthetic is withdrawn and the person is moved to a recovery area. The theatre team clean the theatre and prepare for the next patient, including laying out the relevant materials for the procedure.

Theatre time costs around £1,200 an hour in the UK ($1,450) and services need to maximise the use of the time and of the skills of their surgical team (Institute for Innovation and Improvement 2020). Set-up time can be reduced by several methods. In some cases, steps can be removed, but in this context, it is more likely that processing times would be reduced by, for example, bringing the patient down in anticipation of the team being ready for them. Another method is parallel set-up. The description above envisaged a sequential process, but some activities can be conducted simultaneously ('in parallel'). For example, a person may have their identity confirmed and be anaesthetised in another room at the same time as the theatre team is cleaning and readying for them. The materials for a procedure will often be prepared as a package and be waiting at the side of the theatre, removing that part of the process from the theatre timeline.

BOX 2.3   ACTIVITY – LEVELLING AND MULTI-PROCESS OPERATIONS

In what areas in your service might levelling and multi-process operations be relevant? Would a Skills Matrix help to identify skills and to plan training?

Takt Time Calculation

Process		Completed by	
		Date	
1	Number of Working Days per Week (funded)		*Only include funded working days (e.g Mon - Fri = 5)*
2	Number of Working Weeks per Year (funded)		*Remove total number of defined as Bank / Federal / Public Holidays*
3	First Shift commence		**Daily Total**
	Last Shift end		0:00	00
4	Time first Appointment scheduled		**Hours**	**Minutes**
	Time last scheduled Appointment ends		0:00	00
	Open Hours per Day	CDCC	**Minutes per Day**
	Open HOURS per Week	CDCC	**Minutes per Week**
5	Breaks per DAY (mins)		*Time where NO Service is provided to Service User / Customer*
6	Set Up / Set Down Time / Huddle / Other per day (mins) (Funded)		
	Available Time (Capacity) per Day (mins)	00	*True Capacity (Mins) / Day*
7	**True Demand per Year**		Source:
	True Demand per Day		
	Takt Time (Mins)		

HQIS 2022
Version 1.01

Provisional Daily Capacity Calculations

Figure 2.1   Takt time calculation form

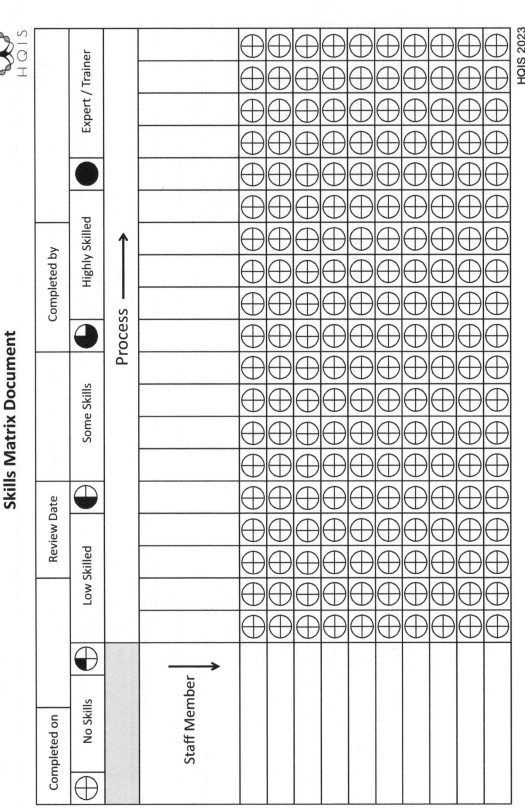

Figure 2.2 Skills matrix

Building Quality into the System

Getting things right is important in any industry. Consumers do not readily return to manufacturers who produce faulty goods, or retailers who offer poor service. In health and social care, where well-being and even lives are at stake, mistakes are still more important. An added pressure is that in many areas of work, it is obvious to the consumer that there is a problem: a Wi-Fi signal repeatedly drops out, an app does not operate after an operating system update, or a refrigerator does not reach the required temperature. In health and social care services, service users will often not be able to make a reasoned judgement on service quality, other than customer service aspects. For example, what tests should a doctor perform in a particular situation? What assessments should the Social Worker make? What type of hip operation should the surgeon perform? In many cases, it will be impractical for the patient to have an informed opinion on the process.

Information for patients and service users is better than ever before, and it is possible to access information online on many aspects of care, and care standards. When people are ill or distressed, however, they often do not take steps to access this. Power imbalances and sometimes local custom make it difficult for people to question what a health or social care professional is doing. The service user may be worried about disrupting the relationship they have with the professional by suggesting a lack of trust. In other instances, the technical knowledge required to make a judgement is so large that patients almost always rely on the advice of the professionals involved.

One way of assessing whether the best practice has been followed or errors have occurred is by the routine audit of clinical records. Many aspects of health and social care cannot be audited, however, unless the observer can be in the same room as the interaction happens. Exactly what advice was offered? What warnings were given about side effects or interactions? What questions were asked in the assessment? Did the assessment take careful account of individual personal circumstances?

Some of this can be assessed from case note review, but assessing the quality of care from written records is very difficult, and usually happens long after the recorded events have occurred. It is impossible to envisage a system where every interaction is observed by another person. Even if it could be, it would be difficult to have a standard for every interaction. In many circumstances in health and social care, the only people who know what happened are the service provider and the service user. Also, by the time a defect in care is identified by the retrospective audit, harm may already have occurred to the service user. This means that retrospectively identifying quality is of limited value. Staff must be supported to make the best possible intervention every time. These practical issues have led to the introduction of Lean healthcare of several other concepts, including Standard Work, 5S, Error-Proofing and Plan-Do-Study-Act (PDSA) cycles. These key concepts are explored in greater detail below.

Standard Work

The idea of Standard Work often makes health and social care staff anxious. They worry that it will mean a loss of individualised care and that they will be expected to treat people as if they are cars on a production line. These are reasonable concerns and follow from fears that Standard Work will be imposed and can never be varied. For Standard Work to be effective, it must address these worries.

Standard Work is a team or service's own view of the current best way of doing something. It is not set in concrete. It can and should be changed and revised over time by the team, based on evidence from PDSA cycles, as discussed later in this chapter.

Teams and individual practitioners often have differing practices. This can include what is included in an assessment, what tests are requested, what information is recorded, who else is informed of what has happened, and so on. Some variation relates to the person for whom they are caring and is a response to individual differences in circumstance or condition. Other differences are differences in the preference of individual staff members, based on training, experience or what they know about new developments in their field of practice.

Staff always need to be able to adapt to the patient or client with whom they are working. However, other types of variation cause problems for teams and service users. It is common to come across teams where administrative staff struggle to cope with differences in preference between clinicians or other specialist staff. Some clinicians want specific information to be provided to their patients, others want a different set of information given to someone with the same condition. They may like their appointments made in different ways or have different recording practices. When the staff member is on leave, it can be very difficult for others to follow up on a treatment plan in their caseload, because information cannot be located, or it is difficult to understand exactly what notes mean, or what interventions are currently being undertaken.

When there is no agreement on Standard Work, it is easy for errors to occur. If surgeons have different practices for pre-operative preparation, it is easy for confusion to happen regarding who has had what treatment, and when. Junior staff may be afraid to do anything at all in case they follow the 'wrong' set of practices and are taken to task for it.

One of the greatest barriers to Standard Work is an unwillingness to have difficult conversations and to challenge cherished beliefs. Even when the root cause of a problem is understood, staff may not be comfortable in confronting it. Where teams overcome this, and mutually agree on Standard Work, it becomes much easier to induct new staff, because it is straightforward to explain the current practice in the team. Junior staff can proceed with confidence that they are doing what is expected of them. Where a patient or service user needs a different approach, it is easy to record what differs from the Standard Work, and why it is being varied. Error checking also becomes easier because there is an agreement on what is best practice.

Standard Work also provides a base from which to build further improvement. Services often change procedures based on a hunch that the new process will be better. Where there is Standard Work, it is easier to identify what change is being considered, how it differs from the current process, and to test out a new process, using PDSA cycles, and subsequently to decide whether the change is indeed an improvement.

A Standard Work description usually includes:

■ A description of the task
■ Which staff group will usually carry it out
■ What equipment and supplies are needed for the task
■ Approximately how long it is expected to take

Standard Work increases productivity by making it clear what supplies are needed, based on tools such as 5S and visual controls, which can make this easier to deliver. An example of a Standard Work form is shown in Figure 2.3. Organisations may have a preferred form for this purpose, often termed a 'Standard Operating Procedure', and if so, it can often be adapted for the purpose without requiring a change to a form which is already familiar to the service.

Staff can be very wary of agreeing on Standard Work. This can be addressed in part by an understanding that Standard Work is not set in stone: it is the best way of undertaking a process, agreed upon by the team, until the team identifies an improvement, tests it using PDSA cycles, and revises and updates the Standard Work.

Our experience is that when teams are given genuine assurance that they can both develop and revise Standard Work, this is often a key step in them gaining confidence in and embracing the method. To retain that trust, any future changes must be tested and shown to be an improvement, but when this is done, the team can alter the process with confidence and an appropriate sense of achievement.

BOX 2.4 ACTIVITY – STANDARD WORK

Which of your activities might benefit from Standard Work? How can you create a culture where Standard Work is enthusiastically embraced by the relevant teams or services?

5S

5S is an acronym for the consecutive use of a series of processes: Sort, Set in Order, Sweep, Standardise and Sustain. It is a process designed to ensure that the right equipment and supplies are in the right place at the right time and are easy to find. 5S supports processes, so deciding on Standard Work makes 5S easier to undertake. 5S is conducted with a team, rather than by one individual. In greater detail, the steps are:

Sort: Separate necessary items from unnecessary items. This needs to start by asking how often items are used, or even if they are used at all. If they are used, decide on the quantities required. For items that appear to be unnecessary, place them in a Red Tag area, where they can be left for an agreed period until the team is content that they are not required, when they can be disposed of. Knowing that there will be an opportunity to retrieve an item if it proves to be immediately necessary often helps people to make the decision that it can be removed.

Set in order: This stage focuses on working out where the items that are regularly needed should be located. The approach is to decide who uses each item, where the item is used, what items are used together, in which order items are used and which items are used most frequently. This information is used to decide where to locate each item so that it best supports the processes that are used by the service. This stage may involve labelling the locations of each of the items and the use of visual controls such as Shadow Boards. A Shadow Board is a series of outlines in diagrammatic form for each item, for example at the bottom of a drawer, which marks out the location where each item is to be stored.

Sweep: Keeping the new storage system in operation requires effort. The service must establish a way of checking that items are in the chosen place, and in the correct quantity. The staff need to identify regular ways of checking on item locations. This is much more likely to happen if staff understand the reasons

Standard Work Form

HQIS

Process Name	
Location / Department	
Completed by	
Date Completed	Agreed Review Date

Step	Brief Description of Activity	Equipment Required	Operator	Cycle Time (Mins)

HQIS 2023
Version 1.01

Figure 2.3   Standard Work form

for the approach and have been involved in deciding where items are located.

Regular checking of the storage system as part of this stage also has a preventative element. If items are consistently found located in the 'wrong' place, this may mean that the use of the system has not been fully understood, or the importance of returning items to their correct storage location immediately after use may be unclear to some staff members. This can provide an opportunity for reinforcing previous learning or indicate changes that should be made to the storage system.

Photographs and diagrams can help to make it easy for staff to see where things should be located and reduce the effort required to undertake a regular check of the storage system.

The Sweep stage includes identifying staff roles and responsibilities for undertaking the regular checking, and will often include a Sweep rota, showing who is due to check which area each day.

Standardise: This stage involves developing Standard Work for the relevant 5S programme. This will include visual controls such as Shadow Boards, photographs, diagrams and Kanban (a card used as a visual indication of what supplies are needed). Checklists can be used, when necessary, but they should be straightforward to use and understand. Communication across teams and shifts will often be part of this, as any later changes must work for all those using the area.

Kanban in health and social care are often used as part of stock control. By controlling re-ordering their use helps to ensure an adequate supply of a particular item, without resorting to over-stocking of that item. Kanban can be used to indicate what volume of an item should be ordered and where it should be placed when the item arrives. They are usually attached to the item and when the item is used, they are placed in a location for re-ordering. A review of the rate of use of an item is required to ensure that the number of items stored is balanced against the re-ordering time to ensure a constant supply. An example of a Kanban is shown in Figure 2.4.

Sustain: Teams usually enjoy undertaking 5S, and the system works well at first. Sustaining the system over time is harder work. Being clear about the relative responsibilities of everyone involved and incorporating them into higher level processes such as Daily Management and Leader Standard Work, discussed later in this chapter, are helpful in keeping things going over time. A regular walk through the storage area by the relevant manager, and opportunities for staff from different work areas to look at one

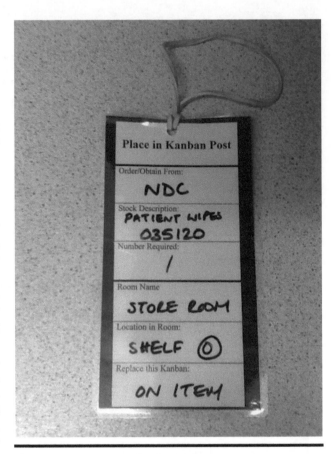

Figure 2.4   An example of a Kanban

another's systems, can be helpful in sustaining good stock control as well as being a good opportunity to exchange ideas. Some organisations use a formal 5S audit, repeated at agreed intervals or when further input may be needed.

Error-Proofing

In Error-Proofing, the team works to reduce the likelihood of errors occurring; to make errors visible; to create systems to prevent errors that do occur from becoming defects in care; to use information on errors to investigate the causes, and to test revised processes to reduce the probability of the same errors re-occurring.

These are a set of principles that can be applied to any system, rather than specific techniques. Root cause analysis is often applied to problems to help to identify the most distal cause, rather than a proximal cause that may itself be a symptom of another problem. For example, errors in a case record may prove to be related to problems in data transfer between systems, rather than to faulty recording. Focusing on a recording problem would miss the fact that the errors occurred when data was moved between two databases, rather than an error made by a staff member.

Looking at the circumstances of errors is also useful. Some situations increase the likelihood of error, including distraction, competing demands, confusing labelling, two service users with similar names and so on. Some of these circumstances can be reduced by careful attention, but some will still occur, such as people with similar names. As this is a predictable occurrence, the system can be altered to take account of the possibility, for example, by routinely including the fact that there are two patients with similar names in safety briefings, or by alerts on information systems.

In quality improvement, the '*Five Whys*' method is often used. This involves asking '*why did this happen?*' repeatedly until the root cause is reached. There is no rule about the number five – in some cases, two reiterations may bring the team to the likely cause. In other instances, a larger number of repetitions may be required to reach the base cause of the problem.

The attitude used in Error-Proofing is important. One of the most important sources of information on errors is knowledge of errors that have already happened. If the management response to an error is aimed at identifying an individual to blame, staff will be reluctant to reveal an error for fear of the consequences. If teams and managers make it clear through both words and actions that they want to get to the cause of the problem and accept that most problems occur because of faulty processes, staff are more likely to be open about problems, and to help to investigate and successfully address the cause.

Despite the best processes, errors will occur from time to time. Making the error as visible as possible is important. If there are key steps in a process where there is a risk, it is worth asking a team how they could make sure that they knew that a problem had occurred. This may be by means of checks at the next stage of the process, for example.

When causes of errors are identified, and possible responses developed, it is common for teams to put countermeasures in place based on opinion, without then checking their impact. Plan-Do-Study-Act (PDSA) cycles should be used to introduce the change and to make sure that they work in practice. Balancing measures, discussed later in the chapter, can also be used to look out for any possible unintended consequences of the change. The discipline of using improvement cycles to test change, and to identify its success and the need for any further change, is a core component of quality improvement work.

Common responses to error are to alter the process to make the error less likely to occur, usually with altered Standard Work. In some cases, inspection may be added. Inspection can be done by the person undertaking the task, who checks that they have undertaken all the necessary actions, so inspection is not necessarily intrusive.

To undertake their own inspection, a member of staff must know what actions are expected of them. This clarity regarding the required steps in the process is one of the core functions of Standard Work.

Sequential inspection can be used, where the next person in a process checks that all the required actions have occurred in the last stage. The principle is to avoid passing an error on to later stages of the process. This is because it is usually easier to resolve a problem if it is identified early. It is also more straightforward to establish the cause if it is identified close to the stage it happened. Unidentified errors can also result in later work that has to be re-done, and this can be avoided by taking corrective action as early as possible. Self-inspection and sequential inspection can be combined in the same process with the first person checking their own work, and the next person in the process confirming that the relevant activities have occurred. This is not a search for blame, but rather to ensure that any error that does occur does not result in a defect in care.

Final or judgement inspections occur late in a process as the name suggests. Surgical pauses are an example of a final check. The operating theatre team pause before undertaking the procedure to check that everything is in place for the operation, and that the correct procedure is being conducted on the right individual. This is obviously sensible as a final check to avoid harm occurring but identifying an error at this late stage could cause significant disadvantages to the patient. If possible, it is better to identify the problem earlier, and to correct it before the person arrives in the operating theatre.

Services can collect data and show changes over time. This is a useful discipline which is used in many change projects. The downside is that the information, if much delayed from the time of the events, may only tell you that you had a problem a month ago, but not necessarily why. In practice, combining early identification of error through inspection at the time of the activity with longer-term monitoring often proves a valuable combination.

In Lean, with its focus on respect for staff, it is usual to avoid having people watching machines in case they go wrong. The preferred approach for automated processes is to create machines which can identify when an error has occurred, pause the process, and alert an operator to come and correct the problem. This is known as autonomation. There are numerous examples of the use of this technique in healthcare, such as syringe pumps which stop if an error is detected, and alert staff members, usually by means of an audible alarm. This removes the need for the syringe pump to be constantly under observation and reduces the likelihood of adverse effects by pausing the process until a staff member can assess the problem.

In some cases, safety devices can be created that prevent an error from occurring. These range from the very simple, such as a barrier which stops staff from coming into contact with a hot surface, to more complex, such as prescribing systems which alert staff to drug interactions and unusual dosages. For a more detailed discussion of Error-Proofing, see Stark and Hookway (2019), and Graban (2017).

Plan-Do-Study-Act Cycles

Plan-Do-Study-Act (PDSA) cycles are an essential feature of quality improvement methods in almost all systems. They support reflective practice and enable the explicit testing of the benefits of a change in a process.

If a root cause analysis identifies a problem, there may be several possible countermeasures. It is good practice to prioritise these options as a team. Considering how large a beneficial impact the change is likely to have in relation to the problem, and how difficult each possible change will be to implement, are key factors that can help to decide relative priorities. This is particularly effective when conducted as a team discussion.

For example, a team may decide to make one difficult change because they believe it will have a very large beneficial impact on the quality of patient care. On the other hand, they may decide that several smaller changes, which will be easier to achieve, and faster to undertake, may be a better place to start. There may be no clear answer to which option is best, but deciding as a team helps to keep people 'on side' with changes, and to create a good collective understanding of why specific changes are being trialled. The key steps in any PDSA cycle are outlined below.

Plan: When planning a change, the team need to agree with the aim of the change, the things they expect to improve, the precise nature of the change being tested and how they will measure the impact of the change.

Being clear on what improvement is being sought helps to keep the team together. If people understand the problem, the reason for the change, and the process being used to assess impact, they are more likely to engage with the work and persevere over time. Figure 2.5 shows an example of a PDSA form that can be used to help structure a PDSA cycle.

Across healthcare systems, it has historically been common to see teams make changes without being certain whether the change produced any improvement. Making a prediction of the anticipated effect of the change and agreeing on how to measure the impact of the change helps to avoid this. The change should be clear, and there should be agreement on who will conduct the change, in what setting and over what timescale. When agreeing measurements, it is important to think about 'balancing measures' as well as 'process' and 'outcome' measures (Box 2.5).

Do: Conduct the change. It is best to conduct a test of a change in one place with one staff member and one patient or process as a first step. Later cycles can be expanded to look at, for example, several patients and then several staff members. Additional settings can be added later. The outcome should be recorded in the manner agreed.

Study: Compare the measured change, and any qualitative feedback, to what was expected. Did the change deliver the anticipated result? Also review the feedback from patients and staff members.

This involves comparing the measured change to what was expected. Did the change deliver the anticipated result? If the desired improvement was not achieved, consider why this might have been the case, and what could be changed during a further step in the PDSA cycle.

Qualitative feedback on the process can also be very helpful, based on asking a range of questions. What are the reflections of those involved – both patients and members of staff? It is common to find additional insights that were not anticipated, and which may require changes. For example, a new process may not work as expected, supplies may be difficult to locate, there may be interruptions or patients may find the new process confusing.

Act: Consider what needs to happen next. If the change did not deliver the anticipated results, consider what needs to change for the next trial. If the change was positive, decide whether it can be scaled up to benefit more patients by involving more staff members or by spreading the learning to other areas.

BOX 2.5 TYPES OF MEASUREMENT

Process measures: Measurements which describe the operation of the process, such as the time taken, the proportion of patients in whom a safety measure is undertaken, or the proportion of patients who report understanding the information provided.

Outcome measures: These describe the aim, such as a reduced length of stay for patients or reduced error rates. Most PDSA cycles will not measure these as they will focus on process changes that are intended, in the longer term, to produce the outcome change.

Balancing measures: These describe any unintended consequence of the work, such as increased staff time for the new process, or any other complication that staff envisage as a potential problem.

Management Systems

For changes to be maintained, management attention and engagement are important. Management systems

PDSA Tracker

Cycle Number

Project Title		Area of Work	
Completed by		Start Date	End Date

PLAN	Plan the change that you want to put in place. Predict what wil happen in this cycle. Decide how you will collect data. Agree on timescales, roles and location

DO	Make the change, remembering to measure and gather your data as agreed

STUDY	What happened and what did you learn? Review your data pre and post PDSA cycle. Did your predictions match the results?

ACT	Do you need to PLAN another cycle? If so, what will you change? It may be that you don't need to make any changes – PLAN how you will Share and Spread?

HQIS 2023
Version 1.01

Figure 2.5 PDSA tracker

are discussed in Chapter 13, and several volumes in the recommended reading list deal with the topic, including Barnas and Adams (2014) and Mann (2015). There are further recommendations for works related to management systems in Box 13.5.

Conclusions

Lean is an approach to quality improvement which has resonance with the challenges of health and social care services. Its focus on increasing value to service users, and on learning from staff and user experience, fits well with an ethos of respect for staff. The remainder of this volume considers how improvement events can be run using Lean methods.

References

Graban, M. (2017). *Lean hospitals: Improving quality, patient safety, and employee engagement* (3rd ed.). CRC Press.

Institute for Innovation and Improvement. (2020). *Improving quality and efficiency in the operating theatre* [online]. National Health Service. http://harmfreecare.org/wp-content/files_mf/Improving-quality-and-efficiency-in-the-operating-theatre.pdf

Stark, C., & Hookway, G. (2019). *Applying lean in health and social care services*. Routledge.

Recommended Further Reading

Barnas, K., & Adams, E. (2014). *Beyond heroes: A lean management system for healthcare*. ThedaCare, Center for Healthcare Value.

Graban, M. (2017). *Lean hospitals: Improving quality, patient safety, and employee engagement* (3rd ed.). CRC Press.

Hadfield, D. (2006). *Lean healthcare Implementing 5S in lean or six sigma projects*. MCS Media, Inc.

Hirano, H. (1996). *5S for operators: 5 pillars of the visual workplace*. Productivity Press.

Kenney, C. (2011). *Transforming health care: Virginia Mason medical centre's pursuit of the perfect patient experience*. Productivity Press.

Mann, D. (2015). *Creating a lean culture: Tools to sustain lean conversions*. CRC Press.

Mead, E., Stark, C., & Thomson, M. (Eds.). (2023). *International examples of lean in healthcare*. Productivity Press.

Ohno, T. (1988). *Toyota production system: Beyond large-scale production*. CRC Press.

Plsek, P. (2014). *Accelerating health care transformation with lean and innovation: The Virginia Mason experience*. CRC Press.

Rother, M. (2009). *Toyota Kata: Managing people for improvement, adaptiveness and superior results*. McGraw-Hill Education.

Sobek, D. K., & Smalley, A. (2008). *Understanding A3 thinking: A critical component of Toyota's PDCA management system*. Productivity Press.

Stark, C., & Hookway, G. (2019). *Applying lean in health and social care services*. Routledge.

Toussaint, J. S., & Adams, E. (2015). *Management on the mend*. ThedaCare Center for Healthcare Value.

Toussaint, J. S., & Berry, L. L. (2013). The promise of lean in health care. *Mayo Clinic Proceedings*, 88(1), 74–82. https://doi.org/10.1016/j.mayocp.2012.07.025

Womack, J. P., & Jones, D. T. (1996). *Lean thinking*. Free Press.

Chapter 3

Beginning an RPIW

Introduction

Careful consideration is needed of whether an RPIW is an appropriate method to use for a problem. Ideas for areas that would benefit from improvement work can come from many sources including staff, service users, external assessors, managers and results of previous work. Any area of health and social care practice can be improved, but the method and the investment of effort should be proportionate to the challenge.

There are four main options:

- Continuous improvement work
- Kaizen events
- RPIWs
- 3P events

In some instances, the investment of time and resources required for an RPIW is disproportionate to the scale of the problem. In addition, not all problems are appropriate for quality improvement work. There can be staff tension in an area that needs to be resolved before considering other options. An RPIW can be a tempting solution to staff disagreements, but it is an expensive and not always successful option to address lingering conflicts.

Many issues can be resolved by supporting staff to undertake continuous improvement work using Plan-Do-Study-Act (PDSA) cycles. This has the additional advantage that the same techniques can be applied to other quality issues, so the learning produces ongoing benefits for the organisation. Coaching the team and the team leader may be a more balanced way of responding to an issue than embarking on an RPIW.

If a situation does merit investment in an event, it is useful to consider what type of event is appropriate.

Designing an entirely new service is appropriate for a 3P event rather than an RPIW (Smith & Bartley, 2023). For situations that cross service boundaries or are sufficiently complex, an RPIW is a good choice. If the issue is a more focused problem, then a shorter event, often termed a kaizen event, may be the best option. These events usually last between one and three days. They use the same tools as an RPIW but will be narrower in scope. The approach described in this book can be applied to a kaizen event with adjustments such as reducing the number of Planning Meetings if not all are required.

The final decision on the appropriateness of an RPIW can be made at a Scoping Meeting. This meeting brings together the people who will facilitate the work, with the event Sponsor and the staff member from the area who will see the work through, known as the Process Owner. The Sponsor and Process Owner roles are discussed later in the chapter.

Before the Scoping Meeting

In advance of the Scoping Meeting, there should be a sustained effort to gather basic data and to obtain opinions on the importance of the work. At a minimum, meet with the person in charge of the process, look for basic data and try to speak to some of the people who deliver the service.

Consider:

What do staff believe is the problem with the current process? This will often be related to delays, long waiting times, errors, unhappy staff, complaints from users or insufficient resources to cope with demand.

BOX 3.1 MEETING FORMATS

It can be helpful to have meetings in-person, particularly if people are meeting for the first time. It is also practical to conduct meetings on line using relevant software such as Microsoft Teams. If using an online format, it is helpful for the participants to share documents in advance and to have any new documents available on their desktop or device to share.

The same disciplines on timekeeping and start time apply for online as in-person meetings. It is easier to sound brusque in an online meeting and misunderstandings are more difficult to catch if documents are being displayed and participants cannot see facial expressions and other body language. This requires extra care by the facilitators to ensure that everyone is involved and that participants feel they have had the opportunity to make their contribution and to raise any points they want to make.

The remainder of the discussion on meetings assumes that meetings can be in-person or virtual. The descriptions relate to in-person meetings because they often require more organisation, but the principles can be applied to an online meeting with equal success.

How do the perceived problems affect users of the service? In some cases, a back-office service may be invisible to the people using the service, but there will often be an impact on them, even if the source of the problem is not apparent to any one individual patient. The work of understanding how problems affect patients includes seeking the voice of the service user. This takes on even greater prominence in the planning process and in the workshop itself, but any indication of the impact on users will help to ground the work and to help to identify value.

What would success look like? This is not a question about what specific improvement actions are required, but rather what visible improvement in the services would be noticeable to people using the service. This will usually relate to the identified problems – shorter waits, less delays, less rework, less stressed staff, happier service users or capacity better balanced to demand.

Where does the process start and finish? This is essential information for the Scoping Meeting. A Scoping Meeting is held well before an RPIW to 'scope' the problem and determine whether an RPIW is a right way forward. For example, there may be an issue with waits in a cancer service, but one event cannot address an entire value stream. In the example of a cancer service, the issue could be one along the pathway of: booking appointments; being assessed at clinics; ordering, obtaining, and interpreting tests; arranging treatments; surgery scheduling; chemotherapy or radiotherapy arrangements; psychological support; or follow-up. Understanding which part of a process is the focus of the current improvement work is important. The focus may need to be altered as information is obtained during the planning process, but you need to agree somewhere as the 'starting point' for consideration within the context of the RPIW. Agreement on the specific steps that form the components of the process will help. How this is done is described later.

Who are the people involved in the process? This might appear obvious, but often there are more staff involved than it first appears. In the cancer service example, a clinic problem obviously involves the clinicians – doctors, allied health professionals and nurses. At the clinic itself, there will also be reception staff. Housekeeping staff may prepare the rooms, and supply staff or porters may be involved in stocking and supplies delivery. There will likely be a system to receive referrals, prioritise them, allocate the person a clinic appointment, send the appointment and, in some systems, check benefit details and insurances. At the clinic itself, initial tests may be taken which require transportation and analysis. Arranging for the clinicians to provide the clinic will need staff who construct rotas, book rooms and so on. This is not an exhaustive list, but it provides an overview of the range of staff who might be involved. Not everyone will be needed: it depends on the RPIW process, but the more you can work out who should be involved in the part of the process to be examined, the easier it will be to undertake the next stages.

Is there data, and how easy is it to access? What data are needed follows from the problem being examined. For a clinic system, there may be excellent data on appointment times and numbers. There may be less information on delays in clinics, or on clinics that run late. Cancelled appointment information may be obtainable, but the reasons for the cancellation may not be recorded. Staff satisfaction may not be collected at all, although sickness absence data is usually available. Patient complaints may be identified but there may be less information on day-to-day satisfaction with services. Where information is collected, for example, via an electronic booking system, the routine outputs may not be available in the format that is required. If so, understanding who controls system access and who can obtain and interpret data will be important. This will also help in the

Planning phase to identify what additional data is required and will need to be specifically collected to inform the RPIW.

Gathering This Information

Initial contact is likely to be with either a senior staff member, who has identified a problem in a system, or direct with a service manager or senior clinician who has a problem they want to fix. This is invaluable but will not always get you what you need. In some cases, there is no clearly articulated problem, or the problem, when explored, is quite different from what has been initially presented. This is particularly common when requests come from senior management, who are unlikely to know the detail of the process. Sometimes, the problem that is perceived to exist proves to be more imagined than real. This commonly occurs when a story has been told and retold and has grown to mythic proportions whilst the actual issue is smaller than perceived or was a one-off incident.

To begin to obtain information for Scoping, it is necessary to go direct to observe the service first hand. If the initial introduction was through a senior manager such as a director or hospital manager, go next to see the person who directly manages the service of interest. They may be defensive if an issue has been identified at a higher organisational level, but often they will have a shared need to understand whether a problem exists, and if so to understand its nature. The service manager can be expected to have at least some information on the process to hand, although the quality and quantity of information and their knowledge of the process can vary widely. It can be a challenge to get them onboard if they have no previous experience of managing in a Lean system and are more familiar with management by objectives where a few key metrics are regarded as crucial.

Speaking direct to some relevant frontline staff can greatly assist. This is not an attempt to catch the service manager out, or to build a case against them. The focus in Lean in health care is on shared understanding and collective work to improve services for patients and service users. Asking staff about their understanding of the process during informal discussions helps in understanding the core steps of the process in question. It also allows the facilitator to check out whether there is a collective understanding of the steps in the process. Different staff members can prove to have varying understandings of the process, its steps and individual responsibilities, particularly if there is no standard process being used in the service. Speaking direct to staff, and where possible service users, can also give a useful guide to how likely it is that a problem exists at all.

Once this basic information has been gathered, a discussion with the requesting person (who will probably become the RPIW project 'sponsor') is worthwhile, to check that there is sufficient evidence of an issue to justify a formal Scoping Meeting. In some cases, it may be that a very focused problem is identified, which the service can tackle with internal PDSA cycles, avoiding the need for a full RPIW.

Arrangements for the Scoping Meeting

For the Scoping Meeting, you need to ensure the presence of:

■ The two Workshop facilitators
■ A senior staff member, often a director or other senior strategic manager, who is willing to take on the role of RPIW project Sponsor
■ The person who directly line manages the core staff in the process under review – termed the Process Owner

No one else is essential at this stage. This is not a meeting to discuss detail or to develop solutions. It is intended to produce a decision on whether there is evidence of a sufficient problem to justify proceeding to the Planning phase of a Rapid Process Improvement Workshop. See Box 3.2 for a description of the roles that are normally defined as being required for the Scoping Meeting.

Project Form

It is important to begin to fill in a Project Form for the event from a very early stage to provide a document trail, and to capture the emerging focus of the RPIW concisely and clearly in writing. This documentation will be built on as the planning progresses. It is important to have written documentation, both because it can be shared and because it helps to make assumptions explicit.

An example of a blank Project Form is shown in Figure 3.1.

At this stage, it is likely that the workshop leaders will be known, and that the senior Sponsor and the probable Process Owner will have been identified. The stages of the process will be roughly understood from the work described above and can be displayed to others. It will be possible to provide a brief description of the Current State. The Current State is defined as a clear description of how the process is working at present. The very highest-level target, such as reduction in waiting times, should also be identified as early as possible and captured in this paperwork.

An example of a Project Form, as it might look like at this stage, is shown in Figure 3.2. The form in this

---

BOX 3.2   RPIW ROLES

Facilitators: Two people who will support the RPIW. They will need to make themselves available to provide guidance on the methods used during the RPIW and to provide leadership around the data collection and analysis. Working with the Process Owner, they will make the arrangements for the dates, venue and other detailed planning for the RPIW, and they will lead the workshop. The role of facilitator can take up to two days a week for six weeks for each person, plus five days for the RPIW event, and some protected time (perhaps a few hours over several weeks) for post-RPIW follow-up. In some organisations, the role will be delivered by specialist quality improvement staff. In other instances, managers may be trained to lead events and will undertake one or two RPIWs or similar smaller events a year. Facilitators need to attend the Scoping Meeting and all Planning Meetings and will be present for the whole week of the RPIW.

Sponsor: A senior staff member, usually a director. This person will agree the scope of the RPIW, and the target process measures or outcomes that the RPIW is intended to achieve. They are responsible for ensuring that the RPIW is aligned with organisational priorities. If challenges develop in the process, such as freeing up staff to attend, they will be expected to help by approaching relevant directors or line managers. If there are difficulties accessing information, they have an important role in advocating for the importance of the event and unblocking any obstacles in making the RPIW a success. The Sponsor attends the Scoping Meeting and all Planning Meetings. They will attend on Day One of the RPIW and twice during the RPIW week. They will be present for the Report Out on Day Five and will help to support the team to ensure that the changes made are embedded and followed through after the RPIW.

Process Owner: The Process Owner is the person who is responsible for the day-to-day running of the process under review. This will often be a ward manager, senior nurse or first-line manager. This person attends the Scoping Meeting and all Planning Meetings and attends the RPIW. They will contribute to data collection and have the main responsibility for implementing the changes agreed during the RPIW.

Home Team: The members of the service who work as normal during the RPIW. They will take part in improvement activities and contribute advice.

Away Team: Staff freed up from all other duties to attend the RPIW. This will include staff from the service and other staff whose presence may be useful, such as people from a similar service, or who work in a service that interfaces with the process being reviewed. Service users will usually be invited to attend the RPIW, and it is often helpful to have two people in this role to provide mutual support.

Advisors: Staff whose advice and expertise may be needed but who are not required to attend the whole event. Examples include IT staff, people working in supporting processes which may be relevant, such as laboratory or supply services, and national experts who may be able to offer guidance. Advisors must be aware that they may be contacted during the event and that they should respond to requests as expeditiously as possible. To be as effective as possible, this requires a culture of support for the principle of prioritising RPIWs across the executive tier of the organisation.

Coach: In some events where facilitators are being trained, there may be a coach who is supporting or training the facilitators. The coach will usually attend the Scoping Meeting and all Planning Meetings and will attend the RPIW itself. The coach will normally have separate supervision sessions with any trainee facilitators after each planning meeting and at the end of each day of the RPIW to reflect on progress, provide feedback and plan the next step.

---

example has been completed using an outpatient service. This example will be developed further in later chapters to give the reader an understanding of how the form is used in practice as the planning and delivery of an RPIW progresses.

Running the Scoping Meeting

The event facilitators need to:

■ Locate a physical venue (or online forum) for the meeting and ensure that it is booked. For a Scoping Meeting with only a few people in attendance, this may be a relevant manager's office. In some cases, it may still be best to book a room, or a seating area, to avoid interruptions.

■ Double-check that the Sponsor has the meeting in their diary, if they are someone with a very busy schedule, to ensure that there is no diary clash. It can be useful to call their administrative support to make

Project Form

RPIW Name		Roles	Details	Approval	Date
Service Workstream		Executive Sponsor			
Parameters		Process Owner			
Start Point		Improvement Lead 1 (Facilitator)			
End Point		Improvement Lead 2 (Team Lead)			
		Coach	Yes / No		

Current State	Desired Future State

Target Metrics to support Future State development

	Metric	Current State	Future State
1			
2			
3			
4			
5			

RPIW Team Members

	Name	Role	Contact Details
1			
2			
3			
4			
5			
6			
7			
8			
9			
10			
11			
12			

Advisory / On Call Support

	Name	Role	Contact Details
1			
2			
3			
4			

Proposed Date for RPIW	
Proposed Location for RPIW	

HQIS 2022
Version 1.01

Figure 3.1 Project form

Project Form

HQIS

RPIW Name	Service X - Improvement for the provision of appointments in Department X to meet agreed waiting times for customer base	Roles	Details	Approval	Date
		Executive Sponsor	Charles Brown	*C. Brown*	21/09/24
		Process Owner	Wendy Miller	*W. Miller*	20/09/24
Start Point	Customer entering the Department	Improvement Lead 1 (Facilitator)	Gavin Hookway	*Gavin Hookway*	19/09/24
End Point	Customer leaving Department - post appointment	Improvement Lead 2 (Team Lead)	Cameron Stark		
Takt Time	2.42 minutes	Coach	Yes / No		

Current State — **Desired Future State**

Service X is not meeting waiting times targets

To try to keep up additional clinics are being run at weekends. Funding for these clinics is not in the recurring budget and the service is operating at a deficit

There are often inadequate supplies to support clinics, and vital testing equipment has been inoperable on several occasions this year leading to delays and to stress for staff and patients

Staff morale has decreased. Absences have increased over the last six months and there are concerns about longer term recruitment and retention

Activity levels are not balanced across the week

Customer satisfaction has reduced by 12.5% compared to the previous year

Capacity calculations suggest that the service can meet current demand in the normal working week if staffing is consistent, work is balanced across the week and supplies and testing equipment are available when needed

Target Metrics to support Future State development

	Metric	Current State	Future State
1	Waiting Time Targets met on a Monthly basis	<92%	100%
2	Reduction in additional staffing costs - per month	£50K	£0K
3	Increase Customer satisfaction levels	82.50%	100%
4	Stock Levels (5S)	Level 0	Level 5
5	Increase Staff Training on Test Equipment	<20%	100%

Proposed Date for RPIW	Monday 17 March 2025
Proposed Location for RPIW	Building A - City B

RPIW Team Members

	Name	Role	Contact Details
1			
2			
3			
4			
5			
6			
7			
8			
9			
10			
11			
12			
Advisory / On Call Support			
1			
2			
3			
4			

Figure 3.2   Partially Completed Project Form for an Outpatient RPIW Scoping Meeting

sure that they know that the Sponsor's attendance is essential to allow the meeting to go ahead. As the organisation progresses on its Lean journey, people across the organisation will recognise the importance of attendance at scoping and Planning Meetings. For RPIWs undertaken early in the Lean development journey of an organisation, it is best to make the expectations clear, to avoid it being replaced by a meeting that may appear to be more urgent.

■ Send out the draft Project Form and an Agenda for the meeting. A suggested Agenda is listed in Box 3.2.

■ Ensure in advance that the Process Owner is comfortable with the part of the meeting that they will lead. Check that they understand the requirements and have had a chance to think about any practical concerns that they may have. This may be the first time they have met the senior staff member acting as the Sponsor, which

can increase anxiety. If necessary, let the Process Owner rehearse their section with the Workshop Lead or Team Lead. A key principle in Lean production is that individuals of all levels of seniority can be heard and listened to. Otherwise, key factors are often not brought to the surface early in the RPIW process and reducing the chance of a successful programme of change.

■ Lead on relevant sections of the agenda. The facilitators can agree in advance which of them will lead on which section.

Action in the Scoping Meeting

This section reviews the actions required for each part of the agenda. The Scoping Meeting is important, not least

---

BOX 3.2 AGENDA FOR SCOPING MEETING

Maximum duration of this meeting is 60 minutes

Meeting Goals (Facilitator, three minutes)

1. Review the draft Project Form, including Scope, Boundaries and Outcomes
2. Plan for Preparing the People
3. Discuss Opportunities for Share and Spread
4. Confirm key dates

Welcome (Facilitator, two minutes)

1. Welcome to the meeting
2. (Do not commence meeting until both Process Owner and Sponsor are present)

Review the Project Form (Facilitator, 20 minutes maximum)

1. Review the connection of the improvement work to organisational priorities
2. Review the Current Situation, Boundaries and Targets for Accuracy, and agree any revisions
3. Identify the process steps in the Value Stream
4. Discuss key personnel for the Away Team and Advisory Group membership
5. Discuss the participation of a customer or customer representative during the RPIW

Plan for Preparing the People (Process Owner, 15 minutes)

1. Discuss any additional Quality Improvement training required for the wider staff group
2. Issue the Sponsor and Process Owner Agreement Forms for completion and return
3. Plans for engagement and communication with staff throughout the Planning process and the RPIW event
4. Agree on the method to ensure that all staff are aware of the final Report Out and are encouraged to attend

Share and Spread (Facilitator, 10 minutes)

1. Consider to which other services/locations this work could be relevant
2. Agree on how to contact these groups
3. Consider whether people from any of these areas should be on the Away Team or Advisory Group

Key Dates (Facilitator, 10 minutes)

■ Agree or confirm the Planning Meeting dates for all four meetings
■ Confirm Sponsor availability for Day 1 RPIW, Midweek (Tuesday and Wednesday) and Final (Friday) Report Outs
■ Confirm that the Process Owner will visit the team involved in the RPIW the week following the event

because it sets the tone for future meetings. The preparatory work for the meeting helps to demonstrate that the work is being taken seriously; that effort is being expended on the project; and that effort will also be expected of participants.

Start the meeting on time. Respect is a core tenet of Lean and keeping people waiting is disrespectful of their time. The tone of the meeting should be brisk, efficient and friendly. Part of the purpose of the Scoping and Planning Meetings is to develop a team ethos and collective understanding of the purpose and aims. It also gives an opportunity to coach in Lean methods and to help the Process Owner, and sometimes the Sponsor, to see how organisational alignment can work in practice. Stick to time, and do not be hesitant to move the meeting on if it shows signs of getting bogged down on a particular topic. Be observant for clear digressions from the required topics: there are issues that need to be agreed, and more general discussion can happen outside the meeting, to use everyone's time as efficiently as possible.

The meeting cannot go ahead without the presence of the Sponsor and Process Owner. If it is necessary to delay the start by a few minutes do so, but if either does not attend, the meeting needs to be re-scheduled. It may suggest that the person concerned has not understood that these meetings are different – they are action-focused, and only the people who must attend have been invited. Not every meeting is like this, and it can take people a while to adapt to the new situation.

Meeting Goals

The main task is to check that there is agreement on the purpose and aims of the RPIW. Sometimes this develops over time, but it is important to talk about it to make any problems or disagreements as visible as possible. The purpose of this is not to press one party into submission, but rather to surface problems to avoid unanticipated problems later in the process. Sorting this out is much more straightforward early in the process, rather than waiting until closer to the event or even during the event itself.

This first meeting should also help to solidify expectations of the Process Owner and the Sponsor and begin to think through who will be needed for the event, and what preparation might be required. These are discussed one by one below:

Review the Project Form

Confirm how the project connects to organisational priorities. RPIWs are major investments of staff time, effort and energy. They need to be connected to areas that are important to the organisation, because significant support will be needed. Organisational alignment is discussed further in Chapter 13.

How this connection to aims is made will vary between organisations. Most health and social care organisations will have Aims and a Mission Statement or equivalent, and usually medium term and annual priorities and actions. The direct line connection between one or more of these work streams and the current work should be obvious. In some cases, a problem will have arisen that the RPIW is intended to tackle, such as a flow problem, or a quality issue. It will almost always be possible to link these back to a higher-level action and to a key aspect of the work of the organisation. This matters, because it will help to keep focus during the preparation and in the RPIW itself. It also helps to demonstrate to staff that their activities have importance to the organisation and shows how their work links to overall aims. The Sponsor will note some of these links on Day One of the RPIW.

Describe the situation. What is happening, or at least thought to be happening just now? Managers are sometimes wary of being too explicit in this section. In some traditionally managed organisations, problems are things to hide, because they will bring unwanted attention and blame. In a Lean approach, problems are shared and need to be understood. Conducting an RPIW does not always mean that a 'problem' has been identified: an opportunity for significant service improvement may have been identified. Either way, there should not be a focus on individuals in the Current Situation, but rather on processes and outcomes.

The boundaries of the process to be improved will have been discussed in advance. Check it here. People can be very willing to improve another department's service, and less keen to work on their own. The process being looked at should be under the direct control of the Process Owner. If the Process Owner does not have a significant role in the identified process, then you need a different Process Owner.

Look at the size of the process being considered. Is it manageable? There is a common Lean mantra – 'Inch Wide, Mile Deep'. This does not suggest devoting an RPIW at a tiny problem, but it does suggest that the area of the Value Stream being examined should be suitable for significant improvement in a week of dedicated work. No team, however enthusiastic, can improve a whole service in a week: keep in mind what is manageable. You can sequence other events to target different parts of the Value Stream as required.

Review the targets. These may be light at this stage, as metrics may not be clear. The overall aims – less waiting, less defects, etc., are likely to be clear, but the best way of measuring change may not yet be obvious. This starts people thinking about measurement and can make it more apparent what information to seek next.

Consider key personnel. Who do you need on the Away Team? As observed in Box 3.2, this is likely to include people in roles involved in the process. If it is a clinical process, think about everyone involved. There may be administrative staff members with a key role. Cleaners or porters might play a vital role in the service. It is easy to fall back on prioritisation of clinical staff, and for many RPIWs they are essential, but often many other people are involved. Bed bays do not prepare themselves, nor samples spontaneously levitate to a laboratory. Care assistants may be important in a process, and different grades of nurses. Think in the range of 8–12 participants. More than 12 participants or so begins to get too big. Fewer than eight people, and it can be difficult to split people up into groups to allow different work streams.

Some people may be very important at the margins of a process, or in underpinning technical roles, but it may be unreasonable to expect them to attend for a week. Examples include Estates staff, Records staff, IT and finance colleagues, pharmacy or investigational staff, or people in technical or people who work in services that are adjacent in the process, which deliver people (or tests, or other support) to this service, or take them from it. These people may need to be consulted to answer questions, to suggest approaches to technical problems, to explain guidance, or to undertake small pieces of work, particularly in the case of IT and Estates staff. They need to know that they might be called. The facilitators need to know they will be available, and their managers must understand that they may have to pick up unexpected pieces of work in this RPIW week.

BOX 3.3 INVOLVING SERVICE USERS IN RPIWS

People who use services should be at the core of the discussion of service change. The service is for them, not for the staff who provide it.

There are several ways of bringing the voice of the customer into the room. Feedback from surveys may be available, or you may choose to conduct a survey specifically for the RPIW. Complaints are another method, as are reports of adverse incidents.

Involving service users directly in RPIWs can be very valuable. We have found that their presence can change the tone of the discussion and help people to stay focused on delivery. There is no truly 'representative' patient/client, and this is often raised by staff members as an objection to the involvement of service users. There are several options for identifying service users to take part:

- Ask a collective advocacy organisation to take part. There are often organisations representing specific patient groups such as people with Chronic Obstructive Pulmonary Disease, people with mental health problems, etc., who may be willing to take part in an RPIW, or at least to offer advice.
- Identify a person with recent experience of the service. Many systems now survey people who have used a service, and in some cases give an option for the respondent to opt into further contact. The organisation may have a pre-existing list of people who have already expressed an interest in helping to improve services.
- Ask an existing group to nominate a member to take part. Organisations such as a League of Friends, a Patient's Council, or other facility or service user group may be willing to identity someone to take part.
- Identify someone who has made a complaint. This can be a high-risk strategy, as there is risk of a person focusing only on the problem they have experienced, but in some cases it can work well. Most people who make a complaint will have been interviewed, and if their problem is resolved, and they seemed interested in how a service went about making improvements, it can work.
- For some groups of people, for example services for people with advanced dementia, involvement of relatives may be appropriate.

To maximise the benefits of service user involvement, the facilitators need to take time to ensure that the service user understands the format, the purpose and precisely what is expected of them. This can be a negotiation. For example, a person may be willing to come for one day to give views, but not for the whole workshop. Other people may be willing to come for two days: one to give views, and one to see and comment on the planned improvements. If this format is used, it is important to not leave this until the very end of the event, when it would be difficult to make any immediate changes in response to their feedback.

Having two service users involved can be helpful, both to allow mutual support and to provide some measure of resilience if one person becomes unwell, or if it is not possible to come for the entire week. Occasionally a professional supporter may be required, depending on the person's disabilities.

Some collective advocacy organisations may feel compromised by being involved in the design of the improvements, as they could be later criticised by their members if their members regard the changes as unsatisfactory. The group may still be willing to offer views or to collate feedback.

Payment can arise as an issue. Sometimes people are willing to offer their time unpaid. Some people must be careful because payment may disrupt benefit entitlement. Other people take the view that, if the professional staff are being paid to attend, they should be paid as well, as a sign of the value placed on their input. Organisations will have different policies on this, but at the least it is usual to reimburse travel expenses and other incidentals. If there is to be no payment of non-professional attendees, then this needs to be clear from the start.

If a service user is to attend the RPIW, the preparation meetings with staff should make this clear so there are no surprises on the first day of the event.

The preparation for a user participant has the same purpose as preparation for staff participants: to allow them to get as much out of the event, and to contribute as much towards change as possible. For them to be able to do this, they must feel comfortable, understand what is happening, and feel able to contribute their views and ideas. The Workshop Lead and Team Lead also need to ensure that the way the RPIW is run makes this as likely as possible.

Often two meetings, or telephone or online discussions, are required with the service users. The first meeting will usually outline the issue of concern and talk through the improvement process. It is important that the person understands that they will be taking part in the RPIW as a full member of the team: they will contribute to decisions, test out changes in groups and participate in the final Report Out.

There are likely to be a lot of unfamiliar terms, and the Team Lead or Workshop Lead needs to spend enough time with the service user to give them sufficient familiarity with the names and processes involved. While it is always good practice to keep access to named data as restricted as possible, the service user must be aware that they may inadvertently encounter confidential information during an event, for example by being in ward areas with whiteboards, live electronic screens and the like. Legal and government departments will have different requirements, but often organisations will want non-employees to sign a form agreeing to respect any inadvertently disclosed information. Leaving the form with the person to consider and sign allows them to think it through.

Some organisations ask non-staff participants to sign a broader non-disclosure agreement. We feel this is not in line with the spirit of open involvement, so, while it is reasonable to ask people to keep inadvertently disclosed information to themselves, asking people to not discuss the content of an RPIW at all is a more stringent requirement, and may be impossible for collective advocacy groups, for example, to meet.

The second meeting with service users can focus on showing and explaining the data gathered, and the structure of the workshop. This allows people to go into the week informed about the information, and with a general grasp of what they will experience, and how the event will be run. Reviewing the data can be a surprise to the service user, as it may not fit with their understanding of a process, or sometimes their personal experience. Letting the person see the information in advance is helpful in allowing them to consider it before the workshop.

Think about how you can involve service users. This is an important area but can be tricky. It is discussed in more detail in Box 3.3.

Preparing the People

Consider what work might be required to support staff. There are two elements to this:

- Familiarity with the observation period and their role during it
- Readiness to participate in the RPIW

Agree on what will be required. The Process Owner is likely to know the local context, for example people who have been involved in previous unsuccessful improvement attempts, or individuals who may have concerns over how work might affect their job. Approaches to helping people to engage in the preparation phase are described in Box 3.4.

Training for the Wider Staff Group

The group of staff who join the Away Team will gain considerable exposure to Lean techniques. The planning team should discuss what teaching may be required for the wider staff group. In some organisations with a long history of exposure to Lean approaches and teaching integrated into organisation inductions and training programmes, there may be little required. In other cases, some information may be important.

BOX 3.4   SUPPORTING STAFF TO TAKE PART IN THE PREPARATION PHASE

Engagement, respect and listening are core values in Lean, and these principles are applicable to the preparation phase. Staff members are likely to want to know:

- Why the work is being done?
- What observations are being conducted, and why?
- What other data is being collected, and why?
- How they can contribute their ideas?
- What will happen during the event?
- What impact the work might have on them?
- What will happen after the event?

E-mails and bulletins have value, but personal contact often has a greater impact. Speaking to people reduces the likelihood of misunderstanding, allows staff to ask questions and gives people an opportunity to gauge your trustworthiness and credibility.

The first issue to address is why the work is being done. Most people accept that all services can be improved, but this abstract idea can wither when considering your own service. Very few people designed the service they work in. In many cases, people do not know why things happen the way they do. Often, they have made criticisms themselves. This is not the same as an external person seeming to comment on the quality of a service.

Distinguishing between weaknesses in a service and criticisms of an individual sounds easy, but when it becomes personal, it can also become very difficult. Staff members spend much of their week at their job and have often worked in the same place for years. Criticism of the system can feel very much like criticism of themselves, even when that is not what is intended.

Meeting with staff can help to avoid this, or at least to mitigate the effects. Show respect for staff: they work there, while the facilitators usually do not. They have years of accumulated experience in the service. Making it clear that you respect their work, and that their views are important, helps.

This must be more than lip service. It must be true. The Waste Wheel and the collection of ideas, discussed in Chapter 4, are important and help to convey this. It helps to give staff a structure within which to understand this. Arranging meetings can work, particularly when these are done in a way that makes them convenient for staff and allows them to ask questions, raise issues and discuss the work.

In some teams, this works best as a large meeting. In other cases, particularly with wards with multiple shifts and day and night staff, several smaller drop-in sessions, timed to fit with staff breaks, may be preferable. If staff members are expected to attend during a break, recognise this. Buy cakes, biscuits or juice and take them to the meeting. Make it interesting. Accept that people may need to answer pages or be called away during the meeting.

Observations also give a good opportunity to speak to staff about the project. When you introduce yourself before each observation session, it is an opportunity to explain what you are doing, and why. This needs to be done sensitively: if people are in the middle of something or are under pressure, let them get on with their job. Introduce yourself regardless, even if you cannot speak at any length. There will often be lulls in the work, and you can chat with them then. Observations during nightshifts are sometimes quieter and give chances to talk with staff. Informal breaks might also work, but sensitivity is needed: sometimes staff want a break from everything, including quality improvement.

Do not attempt to hide anything. Respect is an important Lean principle. Part of respect is treating people like adults. Sometimes that can include reflecting back on information that people may find uncomfortable. That does not imply blame, but it does need honesty.

It is not necessary or practical to provide the same volume of training, but some information can be very useful. An introduction to ideas of Value and Waste can be helpful for the Waste Wheel completion. What else might be useful will depend on the event, and the issues to be reviewed. Often some discussion of flow can be helpful, particularly in advance of issuing ideas forms.

A session on Value and Waste can be combined with discussions with staff as described in Box 3.4 and can also lead to a discussion of the Waste Wheel and how it can be

RPIW Planning Sheet
Key Meeting Dates

RPIW Title	Service X - Improvement for the provision of appointments in Department X to meet agreed waiting times for customer base				
Date of RPIW	Mon-17-Mar-25	to	Fri-21-Mar-25	Location / Venue	Building A - City / Town B
Workshop Lead	Gavin Hookway	Contact Details	0123-4567-8910		
Team Leader	Cameron Stark	Contact Details	0123-4567-8911	Stop the Line	if Scoping Meeting has not taken place by
Process Owner	Wendy Miller	Contact Details	0123-4567-8910		Fri-17-Jan-25
Executive Sponsor	Charles Brown	Contact Details	0123-4567-8911		
Coach (if applicable)					

Suggested Planning Meeting Dates (Week Commencing)	Max.Duration	Agreed RPIW Planning Meeting Times			MS Teams Link
		Date	From	To	
Scoping Meeting	120 mins	Fri-13-Dec-19	15:00	17:00	MS Teams Link 1
1st Planning Meeting	60 mins	Fri-14-Feb-20	08:30	09:30	MS Teams Link 2
2nd Planning Meeting	60 mins	Wed-26-Feb-20	10:00	11:00	MS Teams Link 3
3rd Planning Meeting	60 mins	Tue-03-Mar-20	16:00	17:00	MS Teams Link 4
4th Planning Meeting	60 mins	Mon-09-Mar-20	10:00	11:00	MS Teams Link 5

Post RPIW Actions (suggested)	Scoping Meeting Attendees
30D TMR & Report Out	Sponsor and Process Owner must be present at Scoping Meeting and subsequent Planning Meetings
60D TMR & Report Out	
90D TMR & Report Out	
180D TMR & Report Out	
365D TMR & Report Out	

HQIS 2022
Version 1.01

Figure 3.3 Example of an RPIW planning sheet

completed. At this stage, a view of what may be needed and how it can be sequenced during the preparation period is useful in helping to plan the work.

Sponsor and Process Owner Agreements

Not all organisations use written agreements with the Sponsor and the Process Owner, but they are worth considering. These have no formal authority; their purpose is not to throw back at people if they do not keep to them. The aim of the agreements is to make it clear from as early a stage as possible that there are responsibilities that arise from the work. For the Sponsor, they must champion the work and commit to the time required. By the end of the event, and often for months afterwards, they should be familiar with the issues and familiar to the team. The Process Owner must know that the Sponsor will support them and will deal with requests and discussions in a helpful rather than a punitive manner.

There is an additional value to Sponsor involvement, in reducing the distance between very senior staff and the frontline. Their presence lets staff feel that senior management takes an interest in the service being delivered and supports the work. For the Sponsor, it is an important opportunity to understand what is happening in part of the organisation and to hear home truths direct from staff and service users without any filter supplied by mid-level managers. This can in turn lead to other improvement work.

The Process Owner needs to know what is expected of them and to understand that the event is not the entire improvement process on its own. The event certainly contributes to the speed of improvement, but much of the real change happens in the weeks and months after the event.

They are acknowledging both their responsibility to support the event and the harder medium-term commitment that will be needed afterwards. This extends to supporting the team, leading, and staying in touch with improvement work, and reporting on progress.

Giving the agreements to both people at the same time makes a point about interconnectedness and the importance of both roles. It is not essential to use written agreements, but it is necessary to obtain clarity on roles and responsibilities.

Pulling It Together

For the facilitators, Sponsor and Process Owner, it can be very useful to have a single sheet that shows dates and timings. Figure 3.3 shows a sheet that could be used for this. Sheets like this can be made up on a Spreadsheet or Database programme. This example includes links for virtual meetings. If face-to-face meetings are to be used, then this column can show the venue for the meeting.

Conclusions

Scoping Meetings are an important part of the preparation process. The meeting should reach an initial agreement on scope and sets the ground for team and user involvement.

Reference

Smith, I., & Bartley, S. (2023). Improving learning disabilities services with lean design: A case application of the 3P method. In E. Mead, C. Stark, & M. Thomson (Eds.), *International examples of lean in healthcare*. (pp. 131–148). Productivity Press.

Chapter 4

Preparatory Work

Looking at the Process

Start by observing the whole process. This can be straight-forward if the process happens in one place and in a short time. It can be much more difficult to 'see' a longer or more complex process, and this is considered further below. Relevant infection control procedures must be followed and wards and services will advise on when visits to an area are possible and what personal protective equipment may need to be used. If no visits are possible, for example, because of an infectious disease outbreak, active participation from ward or service staff may need to be negotiated to allow all required observations to be conducted.

For a process that happens in one place, or mainly in one place, ask to follow the whole process through. You do not need to have the Process Owner with you to do this and it can be helpful to not be accompanied by senior staff whose presence may encourage people to tell you what they believe they should say, rather than always what happens. The Process Owner should let their colleagues know that observations will be happening and explain their purpose.

Where there is a clinical process, such as an outpatient clinic or diagnostic testing, start by following patients through their journey. Introduce yourself to the staff working that day and answer any questions they have. They should have known that you were to attend but messages are not always passed on, so it is best to make no assumptions. Wear identification and be prepared to explain why you are there to anyone who asks, staff or service user. This approach applies just as much to laboratory or office processes. You may be following a biological sample or a referral request, but the general principles apply, even if there is no direct service user involvement.

Where service users are involved, once staff are clear about what is happening, introduce yourself to a service user who has arrived for the process. Explain the purpose of your work including its intended value for patients and

ask if they are willing to let you follow them through the process. Some people will decline. Thank them for their time and ask the next person. There is no need to attempt to change their mind. Some people may say 'no', think about it and come back to you.

It is not usually necessary to sit in on a clinical encounter. At least at first, concentrate on the sequence in which things happen, the time of each step and the waits between steps. It is common to find that these are the largest issues, or at least bring the greatest immediate gains. As a process is refined, it may become useful to look in more detail at the clinical interaction, for example for repetition in different processes, or for delays, such as results being difficult to find. In this initial period, however, it is usually fine to wait outside a clinic room or imaging room until the patient reappears.

Walk Through

Follow three of four patients through the whole process. Depending on the length of the process, this may be quick or it can take several hours. In this phase, do not record timings. Just watch the process happening. Consider:

- The sequence of the steps
- Which staff members and roles are involved in each step
- The equipment and records, including information systems, being used at each stage
- Any variation you observe in processes – not everyone may be going through the same sequence
- Any safety checks, such as checking identity
- Any initial evidence of delays or rework
- What questions the service user asks about the process

As you watch the process, it is useful to draw the flow of staff, patients and materials. This can be done using a Process Work Sheet (Figure 4.1).

DOI: 10.4324/9780429020742-4

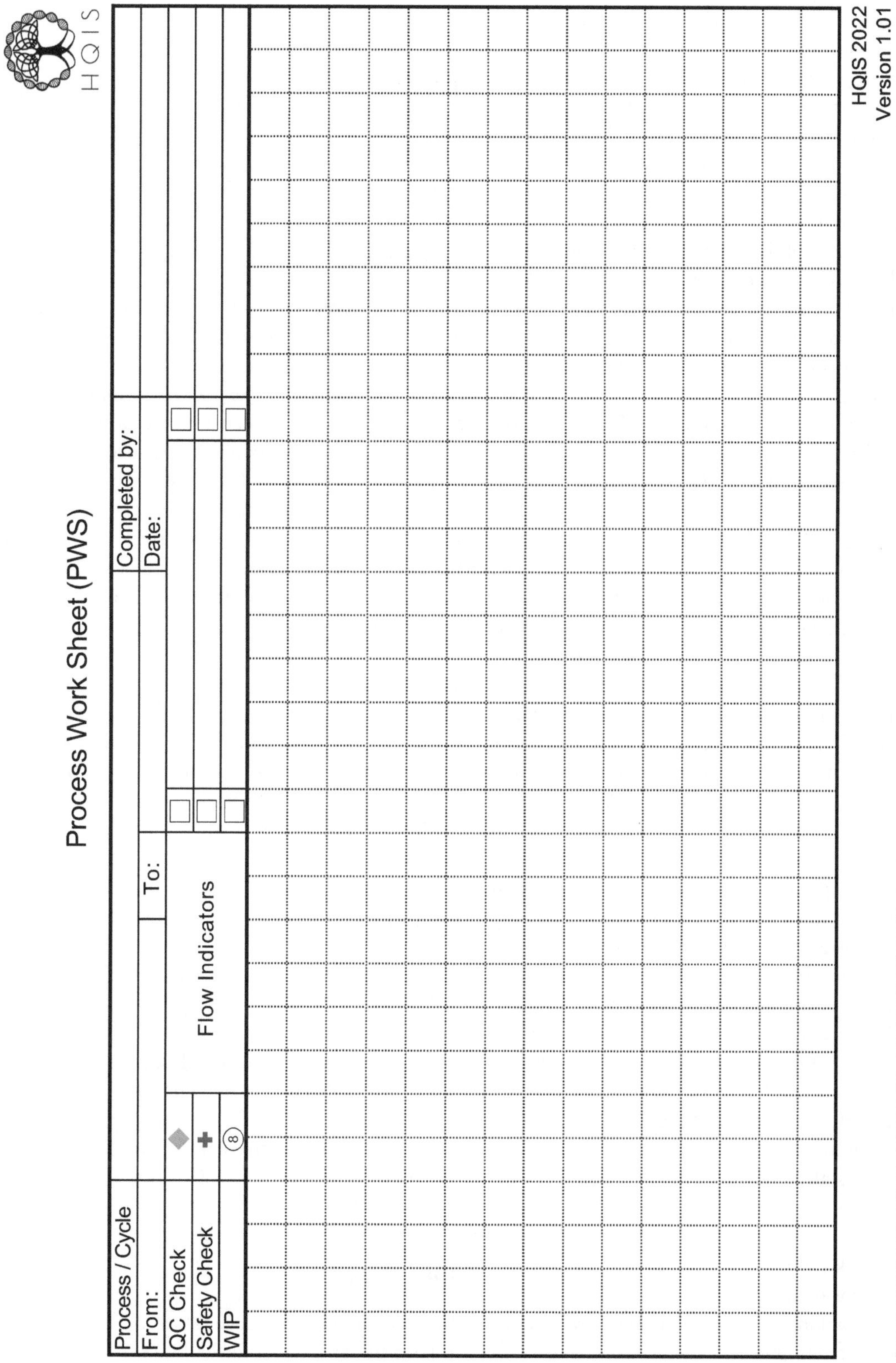

Process Work Sheet (PWS)

HQIS

Process / Cycle		QC Check	Safety Check	WIP	Flow Indicators	To:						Completed by:	Date:
From:		◆	✚	⑧									

HQIS 2022
Version 1.01

Figure 4.1 Process Work Sheet

Feel free to ask clarifying questions about what is happening. This should not feel like an interrogation. Questions like '*what information system are you using now?*' and '*who do you send that form to?*' are fine but steer clear of anything that sounds critical. You are there to observe, not to give the people who work in the service the benefit of your spontaneous advice. Thinking that you have an insight that they have not identified in their experience might be correct – people from outside of a process do sometimes find it easier to 'see' the flow and problems in a process – but do not assume that this is the case.

Clarifications are helpful and can be reinforcing as they also help to demonstrate interest and attention. Asking why something is done can be fine, if your manner makes clear that you are interested, rather than critical. You may also see potential waste. You can ask whether a problem often occurs, such as '*how often do you find that there are not enough supplies?*' or '*how often is that information missing?*' Understanding the experience of the staff, and the things that cause them problems, is an important part of the process.

Service users may be experiencing a service for the first time and seeing it through their eyes is invaluable. Activities that may seem obvious to the staff, or processes that they understand well, may seem puzzling or confusing to service users. Asking them how they find things, what else they would have liked to be told or be asked and how the experience felt to them will be helpful to the staff team. Service users' views may need to be collected more systematically later in the process, but it is best to take any opportunity to ask how the process feels to the service user.

When you have watched the whole process through three times, on a process that is directly observable, begin to draw up a basic diagram of the process showing the main blocks of activity. In due course, this will be used to help develop the Value Stream Map (VSM), discussed later.

Put in the main blocks of activity that you have observed. Note what equipment and information systems/forms are used at each stage and who carries it out. There will probably be variants you have not yet seen, but this begins to provide an overall view of the process. You can also begin to identify variations and problems.

Take this diagram back to the Process Owner and show it to as many staff as possible.

Ask them:

- Does this look right?
- Are there steps missing?
- What proportion of people/samples would go through a different process?

Amend the diagram as required, but keep in mind that a diagram in healthcare cannot cover every possible variant

pathway. See the Pareto discussion later in the chapter. Process mapping with a team should follow observation and is discussed in detail in Chapter 5.

Timings

From this baseline process diagram, decide what timings are required. There are several key measures, including Lead Time, Cycle Time, Wait Times and Takt Time.

Lead Time

The Lead Time is the time from the beginning of the process being observed to its conclusion. If looking at a whole service line, this could be from referral to secondary care because of a possible cancer, to completion of surgery and other therapies, such as chemotherapy or immunological therapy, for people who prove to have cancer. In other cases, it could be from the receipt of a referral to the issuing of an appointment (or to the attendance for the appointment); the time from arrival at a clinic to leaving the clinic; the time from receipt of a sample to issuing of a result, etc. A Direct Observation Record can be used to record timings (Figure 4.2).

Cycle Time

Cycle Times are the time for individual parts of a process. In the outpatient appointment example, this may include activities such as booking the patient in at the clinic, the clinical assessment, an intervention such as an investigation, etc.

Wait Times

Wait times are the waits between cycles. Each cycle may have waits with it, for example when a staff member is looking for supplies, but there will also be waits between cycles. A wait can be recorded as a step in a process cycle. So, for example, Step #1 may be 'Booked in at Reception', Step #2 could be 'Wait' and then Step #3 'Nurse collects patient' or whatever steps are relevant. The sum of all the Cycle Times plus the sum of all the Wait Times will equal the Lead Time.

Takt Time

The takt time is the pace at which a service must work to keep up with demand. Unlike the other measures, takt time is calculated rather than measured. It is worked out from the time a service is open for business, divided by the demand.

Direct Observation Record (DOR)

Scope of Operations	From:									Date/Time:				
	To:									Completed By:				
#	Activity	1	2	3	4	5	6	7	8	9	10	11	12	Mode Time	Notes

Lead Time:
Less Wait and Walk:
Processing (Value) Time:

HQIS 2022
Version 1.01

Figure 4.2 Direct Observation Record

For example, if a clinic runs once a week for four hours, and there are an average of eight referrals a week, then the takt time = 320 minutes/(divided by) eight = 40 minutes. This means that a new patient must leave the clinic every 40 minutes while it is open. The same principle applies to other situations, such as X-ray requests or laboratory tests.

There are two important things to understand about takt time:

- The takt time is not negotiable. It can only change if the opening time of the service alters or the demand for the service alters.
- The takt time does not mean that only the length of the takt time can be devoted to one patient, one test, etc. It can help to calculate how many staff are required. For example, if a process takes 15 minutes, but the takt time is five minutes, then the service needs to be able to manage three patients at once (15/5), which may mean three staff, assuming each person is seen by one staff member.

Figure 2.1 shows an example of a form used to calculate takt time, and Figure 4.3 shows a completed form for the outpatient example.

Measuring Times

It is useful to have the things you need to hand when recording measurements. Box 4.1 lists some of the items that can be used. Some facilitators prefer to use software solutions on a tablet computer. This is fine if it works for the facilitator, but when coaching it can be helpful to start with paper to ensure that people understand the principles.

BOX 4.1   MEASUREMENT KIT

Supply of Forms –
- Direct Observation Record
- Process Work Sheet
- Blank paper (paper with a dotted grid works well)
- Pencil
- Pencil sharpener
- Eraser
- Coloured pencils
- Ruler
- Clip board – a clipboard that is also a container works well and allows you to have everything together (Figure 4.4).
- Stopwatch – people often use a mobile phone for timing, but some clinical areas do not allow the use of phones.

A Direct Observation Record is used to record the timings for the Cycles, Waits and Lead Times (Figure 4.2). A completed Direct Observation Record is shown for the Outpatient example in Figure 4.5. Write the cycles down the left of the form, including waits between Cycles. Each column relates to a separate series of observations. The Total at the foot of the sheet gives the Lead Times for each set of observations. In the example given, the improvement facilitator has used the mode, the most frequent observation, to describe the process. It would also be possible to use a median or an arithmetic average depending on what seems to best describe the process.

Each row is divided into two. Within an individual observation, write the start time of that Cycle or Wait at the top of the two boxes in that row. If a stopwatch or stopwatch App on a mobile phone is being used, the top line will usually be 0:00 (zero minutes, zero seconds). Carry on with the observations, recording the start time of each Wait or Cycle in the top space on each row as you follow the process through. Once you have the whole observation, the Lead Time can be read directly from the last time, if the column commenced at 0:00, or calculated by subtracting the start time from the end time. Adding and subtracting times is tricky, and there are Apps for both PCs and Android and Apple devices that can be used to simplify things.

To work out the times for each Cycle or Wait, subtract the top row of the following observation from the top row of the proceeding observation (Figure 4.6). This gives you the duration of the activity or wait, and it is written in the bottom cell in each row. This is complicated to explain in text, but straightforward to do in practice, and an examination of Figure 4.6 will explain the system.

Look across the observations for a Cycle or Wait to see the range of timings for that part of the process. Modes, the commonest observation in a series, are often used to summarise the observations. An arithmetical average or median can be the best measure in other situations. Look to see which best represents your own series of observations.

As observations continue, it may become apparent that there is more than one common pathway through the process. If a group of service users consistently have a longer pathway because of different needs from another group of service users, it may be unhelpful to look at the mode or even the average. Describing the difference between the two or more distinct groups will often be necessary. Once the proportion of service users who require each pathway is known, this will help to calculate the resource required and to see opportunities for improvement.

Scaling Up Observations

When you have worked out the activities you need to time, consider how many episodes of care/activities you are likely

Takt Time Calculation

	Process	Completed by	Gavin Hookway
	Department X Outpatient Appointments required in a calendar year	Date	5th October 2024
1	Number of Working Days per Week (funded)	5	*Only include funded working days (e.g Mon - Fri = 5)*
2	Number of Working Weeks per Year (funded)	50	*Remove total number of defined as Bank / Federal / Public Holidays*
3	First Shift commence	7:30	**Daily Total**
	Last Shift end	18:30	11:00 / 660
4	Time first Appointment scheduled	8:30	**Hours** / **Minutes**
	Time last scheduled Appointment ends	17:00	8:30 / 510
	Open Hours per Day	11:00	**Minutes per Day** — 690
	Open HOURS per Week	55:00	**Minutes per Week** — 3450
5	Breaks per DAY (mins)	30	*Time where NO Service is provided to Service User / Customer*
6	Set Up / Set Down Time / Huddle / Other per day (mins) (Funded)	120	
	Available Time (Capacity) per Day (mins)	**480**	True Capacity (Mins) / Day
7	**True Demand per Year**	50000	Source:
	True Demand per Day	200	
	Takt Time (Mins)	02:24	

Provisional Daily Capacity Calculations

HQIS 2022
Version 1.01

Figure 4.3   Example of a completed Takt Time Form

Figure 4.4 Observation materials

to need to observe, and whether there are other factors to be considered in recording timings.

Aim for at least ten observations of the whole process. There is no magic about this number. Sometimes, it becomes clear that the process is very consistent, and fewer observations may be required. In other cases, there may be marked variation and more observations may be required to understand what is happening.

Considerations for an Observation Plan

Variations in Pathways

In the initial discussion, during early observations or later in the observation process, you may discover that there is more than one pathway. In some services, there may be several pathways. These can often be grouped up into 'families' of pathways, and this is discussed further later. Where there are variations in pathways, observations of identical processes within several pathways can be used in multiple pathway timings. There may be some activities that are unique to that pathway or to a smaller number of pathways. Specific timings of that activity will be required.

It is useful to separate common variations from uncommon events, discussed in the next section. These variants often relate to an additional process, such as an investigation, or a different treatment. Often these split off from

other pathways because of an assessment, or an earlier test result or measurement.

Measuring the activities alone will not be sufficient. Variant pathways often have the longest waits because the system is set up to work well with the commonest route through the process. Understanding the delays in these variant pathways will be important and can help to direct improvement attention.

Differences in Context

A rural Emergency Department (ED) will be very different from an inner-city ED in a built-up area with a much greater population density. A plan that works for observations in one of these settings will not be interchangeable with the other. Within either site, there will be differences by time of the day and by the day of the week. There may also be differences associated with the season of the year, or with holidays, for example.

Seasonal differences are likely to be impossible to capture in observational data, although they can be identified using other types of data, and this is discussed later in the chapter. It is useful to set out a plan that does take account of the main differences. In the ED example, setting out to conduct observations systemically in daytime, evenings and overnight and on weekdays and weekends will be necessary. You do not need to conduct observations every morning, every evening and so on, and are unlikely to have the capacity to do so. A decision to have a weekend overnight observation session, a weekend daytime observation session, a weekday morning, etc., will be more useful than capturing ten observations all on weekday afternoons, for example.

Unpredictable or Uncommon Events

Staff often want to tell you everything about a process. It is an uncommon experience to have someone ask about your job in detail and to be interested in the detail of what you do. This is great and you should listen carefully. Sometimes people include 'war stories' – anecdotes about events that have stuck in their mind, and that they want to be sure you consider. Understanding how common these events are is essential. Whole workarounds are sometimes based on an event that happened once but that was so upsetting or disruptive that staff want to be sure that it does not happen again. There is no need to be confrontational. Gentle enquiry will usually allow the details to be teased out.

Some uncommon but serious events do need to be included in planning. Anaphylaxis may be uncommon, but it needs an immediate response. Other uncommon events such as weather blocking supply routes may be best dealt with by the wider organisation than by actions by

Direct Observation Record (DOR)

 HQIS

Scope of Operations	From:	Arrival in Department	Date/Time:	5th October 2024 - 08:00 to 13:00
	To:	Departure from Department - Post Appointment	Completed By:	Gavin Hookway

#	Activity	1	2	3	4	5	6	7	8	9	10	11	12	Most Frequent / Mode Time	Notes
1	Arrive at Reception	00:00	00:00	00:00	00:00	00:00	00:00	00:00	00:00	00:00	00:00	00:00	00:00	04:00	Wait
2	Check in with Reception Team	04:00	05:00	03:00	04:00	03:00	05:00	04:00	03:00	04:00	05:00	03:00	01:00	01:00	Value
3	Transfer to Wait Area	05:00	05:00	03:00	04:00	03:00	05:00	04:00	03:00	04:00	05:00	03:00	01:00	10:00	Wait
4	Called to Test Room 1	10:00	10:00	10:00	10:00	10:00	10:00	10:00	10:00	10:00	10:00	10:00	10:00	01:00	Walk
5	Arrive at Test Room 1	15:00	11:00	14:00	12:00	11:00	11:00	13:00	15:00	16:00	10:00	15:00	12:00	05:00	Value
6	Depart Test Room 1	16:00	11:00	15:00	13:00	12:00	12:00	14:00	16:00	17:00	11:00	16:00	13:00	01:00	Walk
7	Transfer to Wait Area	19:00	17:00	19:00	18:00	16:00	17:00	19:00	21:00	21:00	15:00	21:00	19:00	10:00	Wait
8	Called to Test Room 2	20:00	18:00	20:00	19:00	17:00	18:00	20:00	22:00	22:00	16:00	22:00	20:00	01:00	Walk
9	Arrive at Test Room 2	30:00	32:00	35:00	30:00	30:00	29:00	30:00	34:00	30:00	39:00	30:00	30:00	09:00	Value
10	Depart Test Room 2	31:00	33:00	36:00	31:00	31:00	30:00	31:00	35:00	31:00	40:00	31:00	31:00	01:00	Walk
11	Transfer to Wait Area	40:00	43:00	44:00	42:00	40:00	38:00	40:00	46:00	43:00	54:00	42:00	44:00	10:00	Wait
12	Called to Appointment Room	41:00	44:00	45:00	43:00	41:00	39:00	41:00	47:00	44:00	55:00	43:00	45:00	01:00	Walk
13	Arrive Appointment Room	53:00	60:00	55:00	53:00	51:00	49:00	51:00	61:00	57:00	70:00	55:00	58:00	24:00	Value
14	Depart Appointment Room	54:00	61:00	56:00	54:00	52:00	50:00	52:00	62:00	58:00	71:00	56:00	59:00	01:00	Walk
15	Walk to Reception & book next Appointment	76:00	82:00	80:00	78:00	76:00	75:00	78:00	84:00	83:00	93:00	90:00	83:00	07:00	Wait
16	Leave Department	80:00	90:00	86:00	86:00	82:00	88:00	87:00	95:00	93:00	105:00	102:00	93:00		

		1	2	3	4	5	6	7	8	9	10	11	12	Most Frequent / Mode Time	Average
	Lead Time:	80:00	90:00	86:00	86:00	82:00	88:00	87:00	95:00	93:00	105:00	102:00	93:00	86:00	90:35
	Less Wait and Walk:	46:00	52:00	49:00	45:00	44:00	49:00	46:00	56:00	54:00	64:00	51:00	49:00	46:00	50:25
	Processing (Value) Time:	00:34	00:38	00:37	00:41	00:38	00:39	00:41	00:39	00:39	00:41	00:51	00:44	41:00	40:10

HQIS 2022
Version 1.01

Figure 4.5   Example of a completed Direct Observation Record

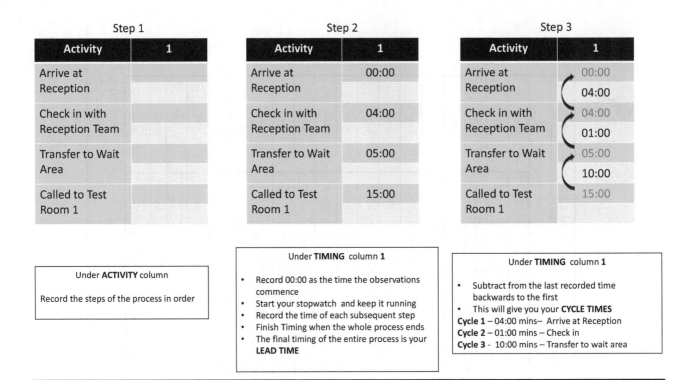

Figure 4.6   Calculating Lead Times and Cycle Times

individual teams, but they live long in the memory and can have a major influence on how a team perceives risk. Sometimes, the story may have been passed down from staff who are no longer there and become part of the unit folklore. Understanding the frequency of events and their potential impact can be tricky but is worth the time.

Some other events are key to the process and must be observed but are inherently unpredictable. These usually relate to conditions or situations that arise unpredictably but sufficiently often to need consideration. This will vary by organisation and by location. A sufficiently large urban hospital may have a steady flow of people with a hip fracture, for example, while in a small rural hospital, it may be a much less common event and therefore more difficult to observe the admission process. Sometimes staff will agree to conduct the observations themselves, and on other occasions, the facilitators may agree to be called whenever such an admission is expected or happening. This can be disruptive, but it is sometimes required.

Undertaking Observations on Spread Out Processes

Some processes are more difficult to observe. They may be spread out in time, or spread out in geographical location, or both. In this case, an observation plan is needed. Start by obtaining an overview of the process by having the staff involved describe the main components. Once the main processes are clear, think through the sequence of observation. In some cases, the whole process can be followed for one case, one referral or one patient. When it is a long process that may be spread out in both geography and time, it is necessary to look at the processes in each location or at each time, rather than following an individual patient, referral or item through each stage.

Looking at referrals as an example, the stages of the process may be:

- Referrals received electronically, reviewed by an administrative staff member, and allocated to a clinician to triage. (Process One, conducted by one person at a time, in one location.)
- Referrals reviewed by a clinician and a priority attached to the referral. (Process Two, conducted by one individual in one location.)
- Prioritised referrals booked into a clinic slot, and a request sent to the patient to call to agree on a time (Process Three, one person in one location.)
- Patient calls to book a clinic slot, and an appointment slot is issued to them. (Process Four – two people involved and happening simultaneously in two locations – the service user's location, and an administrative office.)
- Service user attends for the appointment. (Process Five – one location, although if a virtual clinic, it would be in two or more locations.)

A process like this may prove to have other unanticipated stages. For example, the clinicians may agree their rota, which is then used to populate a clinic template. The clinic templates – the appointment lengths, precise timings and lengths – may also need to be constructed. Clinic rooms themselves need to be allocated in some way, and equipment may be needed for specific clinic sessions and require to be requested in advance. It is not always clear at the beginning of an observation plan what stages need to be observed. Some stages may be important but might remain out of the scope of the current work.

The initial plan should be simple – the main blocks of activity, in the main locations. The same general principles apply. Go to the workplace, talk to the staff respectfully and learn from their experience, and follow several examples through that part of the process if possible.

Work out the time that will be needed to arrange site visits, to travel to different locations and to go back if required. Having two facilitators involved in the pre-RPIW work can greatly assist with this process by spreading the workload. It also has the significant advantage of bringing an extra pair of eyes to the process.

The two facilitators can draw up an observation plan. Opportunity may be more important than seeing each stage in its natural sequence. It is better to see the stage at all than to only see stages in the order in which they occur. Think of it as a movie where filming may take place out of the sequence it will be shown in the completed film, because it is more convenient to do so. The plan may include initial tentative thoughts on aspects that should be reviewed during each visit, which have already come up in discussions, staff suggestions or service user feedback.

Collecting Other Information on the Process

Direct observations are essential but not all aspects of a process can be observed directly. Numerical information is very helpful. It also acts as a check on opinions and perceived wisdom. What needs to be collected can vary markedly between topics and will also depend on the target of the work.

In the outpatient example given earlier the volume of referrals, their source and their disposal are all likely to be relevant. Understanding referral numbers per year, and the pattern of those referrals, will be essential. The type of questions that could be asked, and which apply to most situations, include:

What is the demand for the service? This will be needed to calculate takt time.

Is there any seasonal or other intra-year pattern to demand? For example, Child and Adolescent Mental Health Service referrals often decline during school holidays because there are fewer professional staff in contact with children. In the UK, breast cancer services receive increased referrals after the annual national breast cancer awareness event.

What is the overall trend? It is helpful to know if the demand for the service is increasing, decreasing or stable. If it is changing, try to establish why, and what the annual change in demand appears to be.

Do all the referrals result in appointments? A service may screen referrals and turn some down as inappropriate. In other cases, a referral may be returned because there is insufficient information or some other error in the referral. Understanding errors in the process will allow error-proofing to be considered in the design of the improved process.

What proportion of people attend? Establishing the rate of non-attendance helps to establish lost capacity. Understanding why people do not attend may also identify problems in the appointment booking process, in the information provided, or could be a sign of delays.

How often are people seen in a care episode, and by whom? Knowledge of this allows you to identify the mix of appointment types that are required. It may also identify variance in clinical practice, which can lead to a profitable discussion with clinicians.

What is the mix of conditions referred? The pattern of referrals can help to identify 'families' of patients with similar needs, or at least similar paths through the service. This also allows the service to find out the relative proportions of demand attributed to different conditions/processes.

Is information available on service user opinions of the service? Many services survey service users, and this can provide a rich vein of information on how people experience the service.

Are there known problems? Information on this can come from complaints and from incident reports by staff. Discussion with people in the service will provide this as well, but checking formal reports is a useful additional check.

Are there external inspection reports available? Services often take part in external accreditation or audit, and the results of these will provide dispassionate information on service quality.

Is there benchmarking data? National organisations or specialty groups may publish comparison information allowing aspects of services to be compared.

The detail will vary according to the topic, but this range of questions is likely to be applicable in most situations.

Documenting the Process

Forms that are used to describe processes include the Process Work Sheet, shown earlier in the chapter, a Work Combination Record and a Work Balance Chart.

Process Work Sheet

This is a way of visually describing movement in a process. The form uses grid paper and can be used in conjunction with a Direct Observation Record (Figure 4.2). It can be used to layer information, showing different types of flows (Figure 4.7). See Chapter 1 for a discussion of flow and Stark and Hookway 2019 for more detail.

In the example of an outpatient department, the important areas of the unit can be drawn out. (Figure 4.8 shows a version for the outpatient example.) This can be to scale, but that is not essential, unless distances are going to be calculated. It is important that the area drawn is readily recognisable to people who work there or use the service, that it communicates information to people who are not familiar with the unit, and that it includes key features that are relevant to the process. Once you have a version that works, it is best to copy a supply of the forms with the area already added, to avoid the laborious process of redrawing it for every set of observations.

In some organisations, floor plans are available and can be dropped into the form. This is not essential. Hand-drawn forms are fine. Artistic ability is optional: the essential attribute is that the area is recognisable. If a floor plan is prepared it is helpful if all observers then use the same plan to ensure consistency.

There are numerous flows that can be recorded. These include:

- Patients/service users
- Staff
- Equipment
- Supplies/consumables, including medicines
- Information

Not all will be relevant to every process, and it can become very cluttered if everything is added to one diagram.

When collecting the information, it can be used with a Direct Observation Record. In the outpatient scenario described in this chapter, it can be attached to a clipboard, along with a Time Observation Record. The observer could begin by following a patient through the process. As you do this, you can also add the movement of the patient to the form. For example, they may go to a check-in desk and then on to a waiting area. From the waiting area, they may go to an assessment room, back to the waiting area, on to a room in which an investigation is conducted, then back to the waiting area and finally to an interview room where a treatment plan is agreed. Their final act may be to return to the check-in desk to make a new appointment. Figure 4.8 shows a completed example for the outpatient example demonstrating a lot of movement by the patient and by staff member 1 during the attendance. The number of processes involved is also visible.

There may also be multiple staff movements associated with this visit. This can be very limited, when one patient is seen in one room for one sole episode of care, or very complex, where there are multiple movements. In the 'one service user, one room, one staff member' situation, there can still be movement, for example because staff need to retrieve records or to locate a particular piece of equipment which is not available in every room. In wards, a common movement is of staff looking for keys for a drug trolley to administer medication. In an Occupational Therapy or Physiotherapy department, trips to locate specific supplies may be required. For Social Work assessments and similar processes, staff may need to identify forms or rating scales that they do not have to hand. Catching the detail of this is helpful, as it often points to possible efficiencies in the services that reduce service user waits, and often also reduce staff frustrations.

Information flow may need to be mapped, particularly as a lack of flow can cause delays and increase the potential for error. In teams who use paper case notes, getting the right notes to the correct location will be essential. Sometimes notes are moved within an appointment, or to accompany a service user to a further assessment or treatment. In teams who use electronic information, there will occasionally be issues about information held on different systems that have to be combined, or at least both available at the appointment/assessment, etc. Showing how people access the information can help to promote discussion in a team where there are delays or challenges in access.

The flow of equipment and supplies can be added in a similar way for processes in which it is relevant. In outpatient examples where different specialties use the same consulting space, there may be varying instruments and forms that are needed, and sometimes different medicines. These may be available in advance because of an already developed mechanism, but in others, this arrangement is patchy or even non-existent. In these instances, mapping the movement that results is

Process Work Sheet (PWS)

Process / Cycle	Single Customer Flow in Department		Completed by:	Gavin Hookway
From:	Reception	To:	End of Appointment	Date:

Flow Indicators

QC Check ◆
Safety Check ✚
WIP ⑧

APPT ROOM 1	APPT ROOM 2	APPT ROOM 3	APPT ROOM 4	APPT ROOM 5	TEST AREA 1	ADMINISTRATION AREA

RECEPTION AREA

WAITING AREA

STAFF BASE

APPT ROOM 6	APPT ROOM 7	APPT ROOM 8	APPT ROOM 9	APPT ROOM 10	TEST AREA 2	REST AREA	STORE

HQIS 2022
Version 1.01

Figure 4.7   Pre-prepared Process Work Sheet

Process Work Sheet (PWS)

Figure 4.8 Example of completed Process Work Sheet

helpful in showing the effort that goes into allowing the process to happen in the absence of a system designed to support the activities.

The key aspect of a Process Work Sheet is that it is based on observations of real activity and so adds richness to the information that is not available from discussion alone. It will have far more detail of individual movements than is available in large-scale process mapping.

Work Combination Record

A Work Combination Record is used to show how activities combine in a timeline. It has the virtue of allowing the comparative length of different actions to be seen, and to give a good visual impression of waits and other wastes in the process. The summary measures from the Direct Observation Records, and from other information collected, are used, so there is only one Work Combination Record for the current process, unless there is more than one process.

In a Work Combination Record (Figure 4.9), each activity cycle and each wait is given its own line. The first activity is on the top line and the next sequential action is on the next line. The beginning of the next activity is aligned with the end of the previous activity so that the start of the record on each line is staggered towards the right side of the sheet in line with the end of the previous activity. The figures used are the average or median observations collected using the Direct Observation Record. The scale used depends on the process being described and should be recorded on the Work Combination Record.

Some facilitators prefer to give waits between processes a line of their own, as this makes the wait easier to visualise. Others add the waits to the same line as the cycle but shade it differently. As usual, there are no firm rules about this, and what works for the facilitator and the team and makes sense to them is fine.

Within each cycle, the portion of the process which is waste can be shown separately. In a separate column, the times for Value-Added (NA) and Non-Value-Added (NVA) for each cycle are noted down, and the totals are summed at the bottom of the column. Figure 4.10 shows a completed version of the outpatient example. It makes easy to see that there are four areas of significant waits which together make up almost 40% of the total time patients spend in the clinic.

Depending on the scale used, more than one page may be required. Some facilitators do this as a design feature to show the length of the process, the proportion of waits and the scale of waste in the process. Others adapt the scale to fit one page, finding it easier to share.

Work Balance Chart

A Work Balance Chart presents activity by time (Figure 4.11). We have found this a useful addition to a Yamazumi chart which shows different activities for an operator within a cycle as a stacked bar chart.[1] A Work Balance Chart can also be constructed as a Yamazumi chart if preferred.

It is common to have to look at the delivery of activities over time and compare them to the rate required to meet takt time. Figure 4.12 shows the outpatient example. In only two of six days is activity sufficient to meet takt time. The chart also shows that in every case afternoon activity is lower than morning activity. On Monday and Tuesday, a small increase in activity would meet takt time, while on Friday it is apparent that activity falls well short of that required. This information is very visible and forms a good basis for discussion within a team.

Summarising Qualitative Views

Capturing and summarising qualitative views on the process from both staff and service users can be challenging. People often agree on the numerical data but can find qualitative information more contentious. People who work in a process, even when they did not design it, can feel confronted and upset if the feedback is not as they expected. It can be hard to distinguish between comments on a process and comments on themselves.

There are two issues: summarising information and supporting staff to make use of the comments and feedback.

Questionnaires usually have some questions that can be summarised with graphs or tables to show percentage responses. Often there will be sections for further comments, known as 'free text'; as there is no restriction on what can be written other than the space available. This type of response can be tough to summarise, as comments may look unrelated to one another on the first review.

Some comments will be very specific to an individual, but many others prove to have overlapped themes. The best way of presenting these is to group them by theme and either to list all the comments on that theme, or to give examples and a statement of the total volume of comments, or proportion of comments, received on that topic. Understanding proportional quantities is useful for a team in realising the relative volume of attention service users direct to different topics.

Identifying themes requires decision-making and different reviewers may group responses differently or identify competing themes. There is no single way of doing this, and the sophistication of methods varies widely. The analysis can be done as a team exercise which can be helpful in exposing the information to a lot of people at once (Box 4.2).

Work Combination Record

Scope of Operations					Completed by					HQIS

Timeframe							Date			

Takt Time					Data Source					

Process Step	V	NVA	NNVA	One Square	=	1	Minute
1 Arrive at Reception							
2 Check-in with Reception Team							
3 Waiting Area							
4 Walk to Test Room 1							
5 Test 1							
6 Transfer to Wait Area							
7 Waiting Area							
8 Transfer to Test Room 2							
9 Test 2							
10 Transfer to Wait Area							
11 Wait							
12 Transfer to Main Appointment Room							
13 Main Appointment							
14 Transfer to Main Reecption							
15 Book follow up appointment							
16							
17							

Totals	
Value Added Time	
Necessary Value Adding Time	
Non Necessary Added Time	

HQIS 2022
Version 1.01

Figure 4.9 Work Combination Record

Work Combination Record

Scope of Operations	Department X Customer arrival at Reception to Departure - Post Appointment		Completed by	Gavin Hookway
			Date	5th October 2024

Timeframe	08:30 to 13:00 on 5th October 20**			
Takt Time	**2.26 Mins**		Data Source	Direct Observations on 5th October 2024

	Process Step	V	NVA	NNVA	One Square = 1 Minute
1	Arrive at Reception			4	
2	Check-in with Reception Team		1		
3	Waiting Area			10	
4	Walk to Test Room 1		1		
5	Test 1	5			
6	Transfer to Wait Area		1		
7	Waiting Area			10	
8	Transfer to Test Room 2		1		
9	Test 2	9			
10	Transfer to Wait Area		1		
11	Wait			10	
12	Transfer to Main Appointment Room		1		
13	Main Appointment	24			
14	Transfer to Main Reception		1		
15	Book follow up appointment		7		
16					
17					
	Totals	38	14	34	86
	Value Added Time	38			44.2%
	Necessary Value Adding Time		14		16.3%
	Non Necessary Added Time			34	39.5%

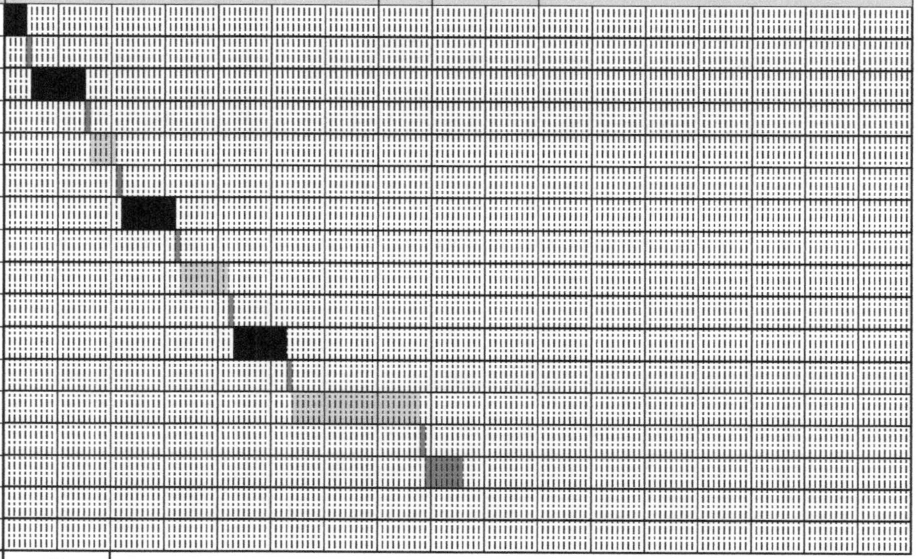

HQIS 2022
Version 1.01

Figure 4.10 Example of completed Work Combination Record

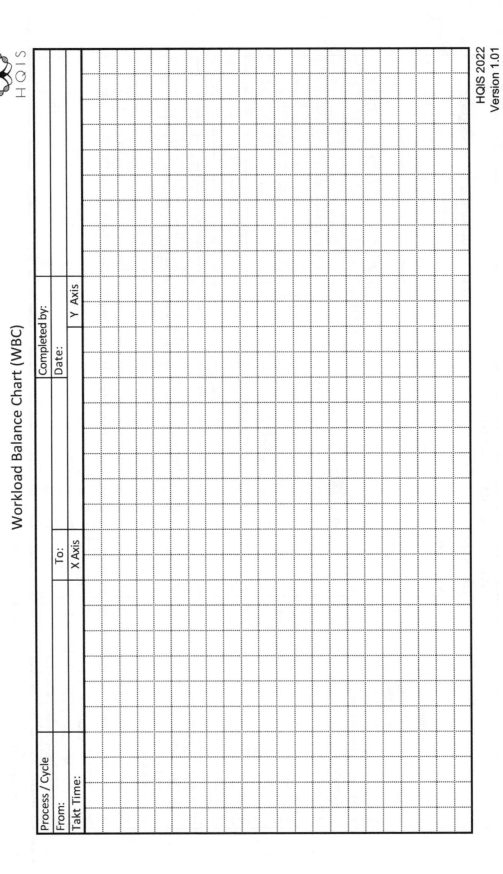

Figure 4.11 Work Balance Chart

Workload Balance Chart (WBC)

Process / Cycle	Appointment Distribution by Day of Week (Average)		Completed by:		Gavin Hookway
From: Aug-24	To: Oct-24		Date:		Nov-24
Takt Time: 02:24 Mins	X Axis	Average Number of Appointments	Y Axis		Day of the Week (split AM/PM)

Average Number of Appointments (Y axis): 10, 20, 30

Takt Time = 02:24 mins

Day of the Week (split AM/PM) (X axis)

Monday — Day 180, AM 100, PM 80
Tuesday — Day 190, AM 100, PM 90
Wednesday — Day 240, AM 140, PM 100
Thursday — Day 220, AM 120, PM 100
Friday — Day 100, AM 80, PM 20
Saturday — Day 80, AM 80

HQIS 2022
Version 1.01

Figure 4.12 Example of completed Work Balance Chart

BOX 4.2 GROUPING FREE TEXT FEEDBACK

Write each of the comments on a card or a sticky note. Where the comment addresses more than one topic, write the different parts of the comment on different cards/notes. Anonymise the comments (see below).

Working with any of the service team who are available, read over all the comments. If a service user is part of the review team, try to support them to also attend if they can.

Discuss possible groupings of the comments. For example, several comments may relate to aspects of the environment, some to information giving, others to the appointment process and so on. Often there will be choices to be made. For example, a point about lack of signage could be grouped in an information-giving set or an environment set.

Using a similar process to an Affinity Diagram can be effective. Once you have a rough grouping of comments, encourage all the staff present to review it and to consider both whether the comments are in the right place, and whether the groupings themselves make sense to everyone. Encourage staff members to move the cards/notes around until they are happy with them.

The process of reviewing, considering and grouping the feedback is useful in providing clarity on where comments came from, and in letting people think through perspectives on the service that they may not have considered. Turning it into a group process with a clear focus on understanding rather than on blame or recrimination also set a tone for the rest of the work.

The approach from the facilitator is very important. They should show interest, engagement, respect for individual views and a focus on learning rather than criticism of the service or of individuals. From time to time, a staff member at a session may disparage or try to minimise or dismiss a response from a service user. The facilitator must make sure that comments are not ignored, and they must acknowledge the validity of the experience being reported, even if it feels out of line with the experience of one or more staff members. Although this is in advance of the RPIW, the tone of response and the focus on listening, reflecting and respecting feedback from others will be important over the whole length of the project.

It must be clear that the facilitator is not ignoring the perspective of any staff members who feel a comment is unfair but rather that they encourage the team to value feedback even if it is uncomfortable. Some feedback can be unreasonable, but if the team starts from the assumption that any feedback that they do not like is vindictive or erroneous, the event will get off to an unpromising start.

Applying more technology to it does not necessarily lead to a more useful answer. Teams with significant resource and relevant experience may use computer software for qualitative analysis, like NVivo, or cheaper cloud-based options like Dedoose, to tag and collate quotes. For larger volumes of data, automated text analysis can be used but this is unlikely to be appropriate for smaller surveys dedicated to one service.

When presenting information and quotes, consider confidentiality carefully. If there are adverse comments about individual staff members that sound worrying, it may be necessary to remove them from the analysis and feed them into the organisation's processes for review of complaints. In other cases, there will be names of service users or staff used or details that would allow identification of an individual. Unless there is a good reason to keep them in, and the facilitator is confident that the service user understood that this could happen and they had given permission for it, it is best to anonymise quotes.

Using Pareto Diagrams

Pareto diagrams are named after the Italian economist and social theorist, Vilfredo Pareto. Pareto never described the eponymous diagram, but he did note that resources were not evenly distributed, leading to the idea of the 80/20 rule. Pareto's work focused on land ownership in Italy where around 80% of land was owned by 20% of landowners. The general principle of uneven distribution was championed by Joseph Juran for use in quality improvement, noting that there are usually major causes for something and a long tail of other causes. The term 'Pareto Diagram' came into common use for a diagram to show the distribution of items by frequency.

The stages to construct a Pareto diagram are:

1. Measure the items of interest (for example, the causes of an error, the number of service users referred with a particular condition)
2. Put the items in order of size from largest to smallest

3. Calculate the percentage each of the items contributes to the total
4. Put the number of each item on a bar graph
5. Add a second axis showing the percentage each item contributed to the total, as a line graph

Figure 4.13 shows an example. There are tutorials online on how to do this on software such as Excel.

These graphs are a visual way of sharing a lot of information in an understandable format. It is common to find that a relatively small number of categories contribute a great deal to the total. This helps to let teams prioritise where they want to focus their efforts. Sometimes a well-known case dominates thinking and can overshadow the numbers. Looking at the numbers and proportions can help to rebalance the impact that well-remembered events have on perceptions of frequency.

In some instances, the work does have to address small volume activity because it is particularly important, very risky or has some other key impact on services, staff or service users. Placing this in context helps to focus people on why they have chosen to prioritise this area of improvement work.

Involving the Team

Team engagement was discussed in Chapter 3 and is also noted here because of its importance. Several parts of the work should already involve the team. In large teams, such as a ward team which may have 60 or 70 staff, some of whom will work part-time or night shifts only, it can be difficult to engage everyone. Existing hierarchies in teams may also result in some staff feeling that they are not involved in quality improvement or are not expected to have, or to offer, an opinion. Part of the ethos of Lean is respect. Everyone's opinion is worthwhile and capturing a range of views is more likely to lead to a better understanding of the situation. It will also mean that a wider range of ideas can be fed into the process. Waste Wheels and Ideas Forms are two methods that can help, particularly if staff have a clear view of why the work is being done, and how these methods contribute to the work.

There are several ways of increasing staff involvement. Briefing people on what is planned, and why it is happening, is worthwhile. This gives staff the chance to meet the facilitators and to question the process. It also lets them gauge how much truth there is in the values espoused. It is easy to say that staff views are important, but people are often cynical about this. They may expect lip service to be paid to the idea, but to be patronised, disregarded or ignored.

The first step is to suit briefings to the context. In a support department, it may be possible to take a large group of people and run a session for an hour. In a clinical environment, this is likely to be impossible. In that setting, short briefings during breaks, conducted in or near

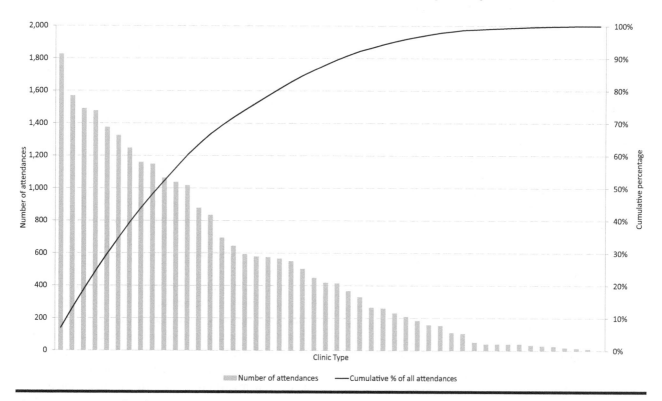

Figure 4.13 Example of a Pareto chart. *Source*: Stark and Hookway (2019) p. 110

to the clinical area, will often be the best option. If people are giving up break time, the session must be relevant and engaging. Where some staff work only at night, briefings in the evening or even in an overnight break may also be required. Excluding some staff only because the briefing time is inconvenient will not produce ownership or even engagement. Well-maintained Team Boards, discussed further in Chapter 13, can be a good way of maintaining communication.

In the briefing, fit the information to the time available. The people running the sessions should discuss why the area has been chosen and why this topic is being examined. If the service is not explicit about this it is easy for rumours to circulate, sometimes becoming more elaborate and disturbing as they gather momentum.

At the least, staff will want to check out whether their service is believed to have failed in some way, or to have some perceived problem. They will usually want to get a feel for the attitude of the facilitators, and how their approach compares to the rhetoric of quality improvement. In some situations, there may also be rumours that there is a major cost problem, and the work is aimed at cost savings alone, possibly with associated redundancies.

If cost is part of the reason to undertake the work, be upfront about this. Hiding something that comes out later is catastrophic for trust and does not fit with the approach of having respect for staff. People understand that the cost of services is important that any service wants to get the maximum value from the time and resource invested. Pretending otherwise will not produce trust.

Go through the reasons for the work and describe the quality improvements that are sought. Link this to both staff and service user experience where possible. Explain who is involved in the work, what the process will be and how the whole staff group can contribute. Talk through the process and discuss the reasons for a home and away team. It is easy for staff to feel that the Away Team is being treated as 'special' and that they are being left to do the work while other people are privileged over them and allowed to do something new and interesting. It can suggest to staff that they are less worthy of involvement.

Making it clear that numbers are limited for practical reasons rather than because of an intention to exclude people, and that people are selected to reflect a mixture of job roles and grades rather than because of special merit, can help. Outlining the key role of the Home Team – keeping the service going, reviewing and commenting on ideas and trying out suggestions – can also help. Talking this through is helpful in identifying any concerns and reduces the risk of lingering grievances. An ideas box/board and encouraging the Home Team to be involved in ideas generation can help them to feel more involved. There also needs to be a

commitment to regular feedback to the Home Team on what is happening in response to their ideas.

These sessions should be as open as possible, with good opportunities for staff to ask questions, to raise concerns and to challenge the process. If Lean is new to the team, then these sessions can be used to give a brief introduction. The sessions should also discuss methods for involvement, including the use of Waste Wheels and Ideas Forms.

Waste Wheel

A Waste Wheel is a large sheet on which people can affix wastes they have noticed, using sticky notes. These need to be large to let people put several sticky notes in each area of the wheel.

The wheel is divided into seven or eight wastes, depending on how many wastes the organisations use. Our preference is to add an eighth waste, usually human potential, to the usual seven of waiting, overprocessing, overproduction, defects, motion, transportation and inventory. See Chapter 2 for more information on waste.

If the organisation undertakes a lot of Lean work, then tough pre-printed sheets may be used to allow for reuse. In other cases, drawing the wheel out on an A2 flipchart sheet with a marker pen works well.

BOX 4.3   PRACTICAL TIPS ON THE USE OF WASTE WHEELS

Try to have the wheel (or wheels if the team works in multiple sites) in a prominent place. This will usually be an area not used by service users to increase the likelihood of staff being open about problems.

Encourage a few people to put up wastes early, to make it less off-putting to post the first idea. Sometimes, this can be done at one of the introductory sessions.

Don't try to edit what is added to the wheel. Our rule of thumb is to leave up any post about the service, no matter how blunt, but to remove any post which names an individual staff member as a problem, or as the cause of a waste. Staff are never the waste and supporting bullying by proxy is not a Lean approach. Sometimes people will add extra sheets with pent-up views. Leave them up – it shows that people are engaged or at least interested in the process. Sometimes people come back after a while and amend what they have written after they have assured themselves that they will not be censored.

Ideas Forms

Capturing ideas from staff is an important part of the preparation for an event. An Ideas Form example is shown in Figure 4.14. The key aspect of an Ideas Form is that it includes both a description of the problem and a suggestion for a solution. It is not intended as a route for complaints alone.

The Ideas Forms can be introduced at the briefings to the teams. Our practice is to make the Waste Wheel available for around four weeks before an event, and then to add a stock of Ideas Forms about two weeks before an event. This gives staff the opportunity to see the identified wastes, mull them over and then share any ideas they have for improvement. Plastic or card pockets taped to the wall beside the Waste Wheels can work (check that the tape does not remove the paint before you stick them up). One pocket can have blank forms and the other can be marked for completed forms. People often want to have a look at other people's ideas and that is fine, but no Ideas Form should be censored unless it is abusive to an individual. All should go forwards to the event. Some teams prefer a box in which they can post the forms but not take them back out.

Creating a Current State Value Stream Map

Value Stream Maps help to bring the information together. They are a good way to show the process at a glance, together with its value and waste. A Value Stream Map (VSM) differs from a Process Map, which contains every step of a process. A VSM is a summary that can be easily shared and contains a lot of information on one sheet. When teams become familiar with a VSM, they can obtain a lot of detail very quickly by reviewing the format. It is important to show the process as it currently exists, not as the service hopes it will be after the improvement work. The existing situation is known as a 'Current State Value Stream Map'. A Future State Value Stream Map will be created during the RPIW. For more detail on Value Stream Maps, see Martin and Osterling (2014) and Stark and Hookway (2019). A blank Value Stream Map is shown in Figure 4.15. The number of cycles will be varied to suit the process being described.

Different facilitators vary in the detail of how they construct a Value Stream Map, but a common approach is:

1. Put the cycles of the process in separate boxes. This needs some judgement on how to summarise the activities. Show the name of the process, who undertakes it and if appropriate, what is required to allow it to happen.
2. Join the cycles with arrows indicating the flow between the cycles. If there is continuous flow, use a clear arrow. If there is a push process, use a striped arrow. If the following process pulls the previous process, use a curved arrow.
3. Put warning triangles between the cycles. Where there are people or items waiting between the cycles, write in the triangle the average number waiting from the information obtained during observations.
4. Draw a castellated timeline below the cycles. Write the average time for each cycle and the average wait between each cycle on the timeline. Use the same unit of measurement for both waits and cycles (hours, minutes or seconds, depending on the type of process). You can take these timings from your Work Combination Record.
5. Add boxes below each cycle showing the Cycle Time, the Value-Added time and Non-Value-Added time, and the proportion of time in each cycle which is value added, calculated as a percentage. It is not necessary to add boxes below waits as the whole of this time will usually be a waste.
6. Draw in clouds above the relevant stage to capture problems identified by the team, and from observations during the preparatory period.
7. Work out the total Cycle Times and Wait Times. The total Cycle Time plus the total Wait Times should equal the Lead Time for the process. Work out the total Value-Added time for the cycles and the total Non-Value-Added time within cycles. Total Non-Value-Added time is calculated from the total of Wait Times added to the total NVA time within cycles. As a check, the total NVA time plus the total Value-Added time should equal the Lead Time. This allows the calculation of the total VA and NVA for the process.

Some facilitators and teams like to produce attractive printed Value Stream Maps using computer software. Our view is to avoid this where possible. If the hand-drawn form contains all the information required and conveys it to others, there is no need to add an additional step. In some cases, organisations insist on printed forms and the use of software such as Visio. If so, its use may be unavoidable but not adding a step that produces limited additional value is an obvious Lean approach.

Figure 4.16 shows a completed Value Stream Map for the outpatient example.

HQIS

Improvement Idea
Tracking Document

Name	Date
Describe the Issue	
Proposal for Improvement	
Anticipated Results	

HQIS 2022
Version 1.01

Figure 4.14   Ideas Form

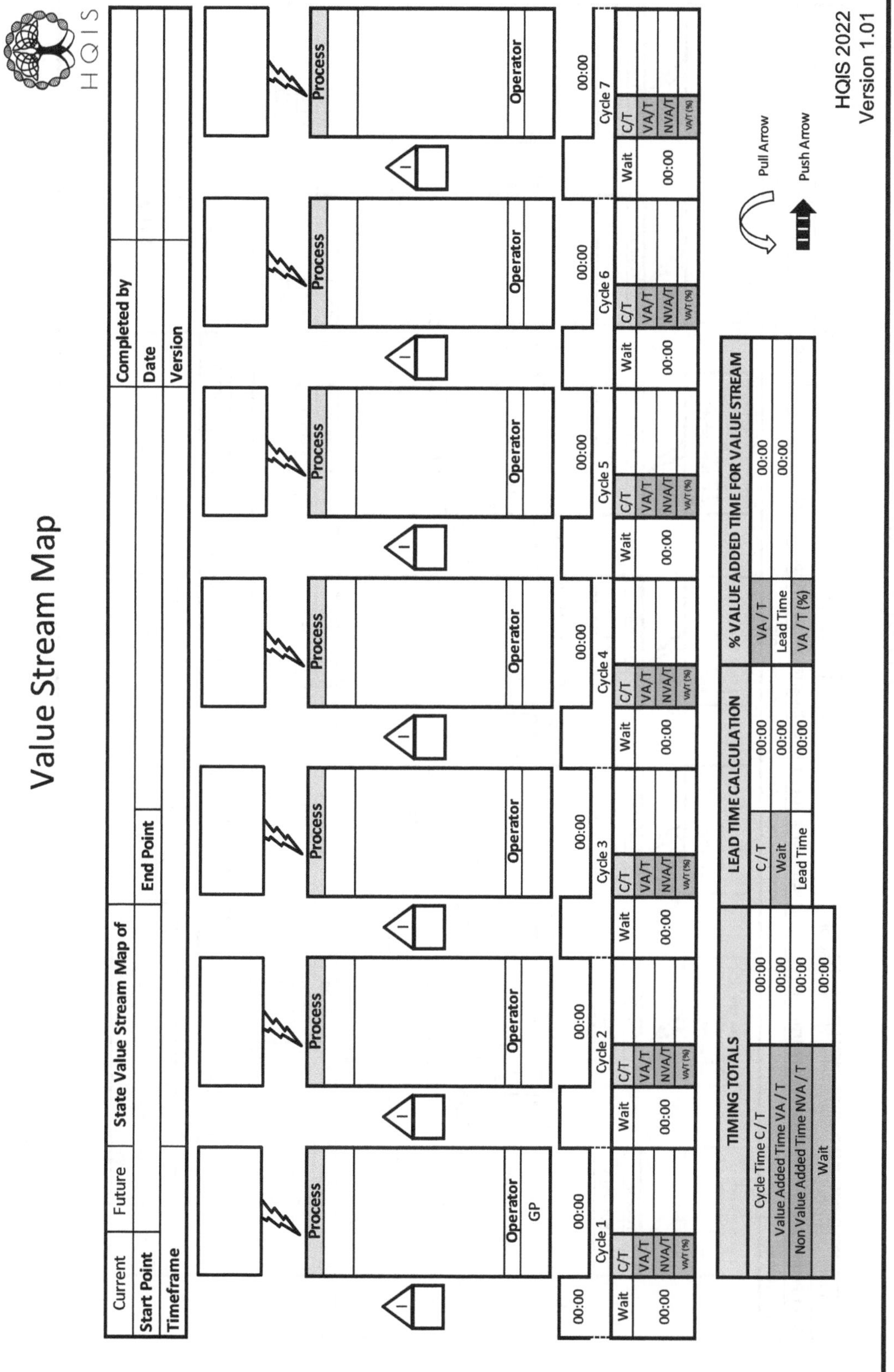

Value Stream Map

Current	Future	State Value Stream Map of	Completed by
Start Point		End Point	Date
Timeframe			Version

HQIS

Cycle 1

Wait	C/T
	VA/T
00:00	NVA/T
	VA/T (%)

00:00 · Operator GP

Cycle 2

Wait	C/T
	VA/T
00:00	NVA/T
	VA/T (%)

00:00 · Operator

Cycle 3

Wait	C/T
	VA/T
00:00	NVA/T
	VA/T (%)

00:00 · Operator

Cycle 4

Wait	C/T
	VA/T
00:00	NVA/T
	VA/T (%)

00:00 · Operator

Cycle 5

Wait	C/T
	VA/T
00:00	NVA/T
	VA/T (%)

00:00 · Operator

Cycle 6

Wait	C/T
	VA/T
00:00	NVA/T
	VA/T (%)

00:00 · Operator

Cycle 7

Wait	C/T
	VA/T
00:00	NVA/T
	VA/T (%)

00:00 · Operator

TIMING TOTALS	
Cycle Time C/T	00:00
Value Added Time VA/T	00:00
Non Value Added Time NVA/T	00:00
Wait	00:00

LEAD TIME CALCULATION	
C/T	00:00
Wait	00:00
Lead Time	00:00

% VALUE ADDED TIME FOR VALUE STREAM	
VA/T	00:00
Lead Time	00:00
VA/T (%)	

Pull Arrow

Push Arrow

HQIS 2022
Version 1.01

Figure 4.15   Value Stream Map

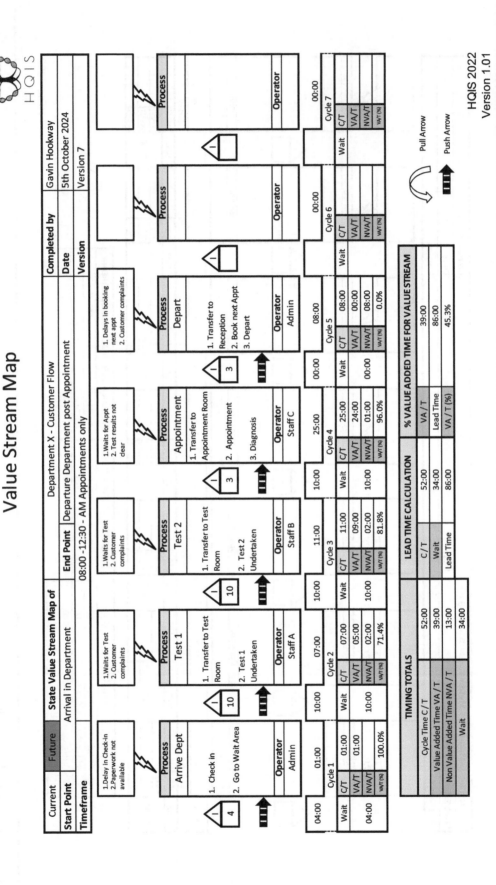

Figure 4.16 Example of a Completed Value Stream Map

Sharing Information Back with the Team

There is no need to restrict access to findings. A Data Wall area in a staff room or staff corridor can work well in increasing interest about the RPIW. Putting up graphs and tables of data, summaries of user feedback, Pareto Charts and Process Diagrams can work well. It is common to see staff looking at these even if they do not raise the topic directly. Often staff do not see summary information such as throughput and waiting times in their part of the service, and it can set a precedent for providing information to the teams. If there is interest, it may be worth summarising at a meeting, but often chatting to staff who are looking at the data wall can work well and give them more opportunity to ask questions or to add their own insights or suggestions

Note

1 A Yamazumi chart is also referred to as a Yamazumi Board, an Operator Balance Chart or an Operator Loading Diagram. It shows the work of a single operator against takt time.

Recommended Further Reading

Martin, K., & Osterling, M. (2014). *Value stream mapping*. McGraw Hill.

Stark, C., & Hookway, G. (2019). *Applying lean in health and social care services*. Routledge.

Chapter 5

Process Mapping with a Team

Preparing for Process Mapping

Process mapping is best undertaken after gathering basic information on the process and conducting at least some observations. This makes it easier to follow what people say, and to have a reasonable idea when something is forgotten. It also allows a modest degree of challenge, discussed further below. This is not an attempt to catch people out, and the tone of any challenge is important.

Process mapping sessions are also an ideal opportunity for staff to record wastes and identify improvement ideas. The mapping sessions sometimes generate so much enthusiasm that staff want to start improvement straight away. This is good but actions may be better held back for the event as the impact of any changes on the overall system may not yet be apparent. If any actions are undertaken after the mapping session, it is important that Plan-Do-Study-Act (PDSA) cycles are used.

Process mapping is easiest in person, but it is possible to have an online version if required, with participants contributing by video. This description assumes the session is being conducted in person. The method can be adapted for online use.

Materials

There are several methods of process mapping. This section describes the use of a Swim Lane Diagram. The materials required will vary slightly depending on the method used, but the principles are the same. You will need:

- Flip Chart Paper
- Thick marker Pen
- Long straight edge (like a one metre/one yard ruler)
- Fine permanent marker pens
- Average-sized sticky notes in at least four colours
- Large sticky notes
- Wool or narrow tape – red, yellow and green

For a Swim Lane Diagram, you need large pieces of flip chart paper or a roll of lining paper. This description assumes flip chart paper is being used, but it is easily adaptable for a roll of lining paper. If using flip chart paper, put it in portrait mode rather than landscape. Using a thick marker pen and a long straight edge divide the flip chart paper with four or five equally spaced parallel lines. The number of lines depends on the number of lanes you want to create. Repeat this with at least five other pieces of paper to give you a total of six identical sheets. You may want to also draw a few others to have available if required. Figure 5.1 shows the layout of a diagram.

Turn the sheets of paper face down. You need a large, flat surface for this such as a large table, or a clean firm floor surface. As you turn them over, line up the 'lanes' and place three sheets side by side. Tape them together using masking tape or similar material. Materials like transparent adhesive tape are not usually wide enough to be suitable. Duct tape works but shows through to the other side.

Once you have three sheets of paper taped together, you can either extend along if you believe the number of people/services involved in the process is small. If a larger process, tape three more pieces below the first three in the same manner and join the top edge of the new row to the bottom edge of the previous three pieces, to create a 3×2 matrix. This is a large piece of paper, so it is very helpful to have assistance when handling it. Roll it up as one extended piece of paper, and tape it with another piece of masking tape to hold it together.

If you plan to run these sessions frequently, look for a part of your organisation that can print out on wide continuous paper. Estates and Facilities Departments are often able to do this as it may be required for planning diagrams.

DOI: 10.4324/9780429020742-5

Figure 5.1 Blank Swim Lane Diagram

Setting Up for the Mapping Session

Aim to have two facilitators available for the session, particularly if it is a new process for the team.

Try to see the room you will use in advance and check that it is suitable. Some of the same things that make a space useful for an RPIW also apply to a mapping event. You need a large wall that people can stand around, and where you can arrange disabled access if required. A small table on which to place materials is very useful. The space needs to be large enough for people to be able to stand back to see it without standing in front of one another. You want clear lines of sight.

As with an RPIW room, check that you can tape paper to the walls. If you can't, the room will not be suitable. Sometimes teaching rooms with whiteboards can be used, as it is usually possible to tape paper to the whiteboards without damage, or at least to the edge of the whiteboard frame. As always, check with the facilities and/or janitorial staff. Explaining to them what you need is most likely to produce good ideas about where the event can be run: janitorial staff usually know every room and are a great source of advice.

Set up in advance. You will need a colleague to support the paper to allow it to be taped to the wall. No matter what you have been told about the likelihood of damaging the décor of the room, check an inconspicuous area with the tape you propose to use, and peel it back off to make sure it is unlikely to cause damage.

The weight of the paper and the length of it will be considerable. Getting one edge supported and straight then allows the paper to be gradually unrolled, supported by one of the duo who is hanging it. Taping to the wall at least at every paper joint is generally adequate. If using a 3 × 2 arrangement, it will also be necessary to tape the edges to avoid the paper turning in.

Set up a table with your supplies, adjacent to the paper. Lay out sticky notes, marker pens and if you want to use it, coloured wool and clear sticky tape (see later discussion). As the work will progress from left to right, it usually works

best to place your table to the left of the wall-mounted sheets of paper. If you think you might need it, lay out some more sections of Swim Lane Diagram nearby so that it can be added if required.

It is useful to have a blank sheet of paper on the wall headed 'Parking Lot'. This is used to record issues that are important to people, but which do not quite fit with the current discussion. It is also helpful to take a supply of Ideas Forms.

Swim Lane Diagrams

At large sporting events, swimming competitions usually have cameras positioned over the pool so that the audience can look down and see the progress of the competitors. This aerial view looks like the basic shape constructed above, so the layout is known as a 'Swim Lane Diagram'.

When using this to map process, the norm is that time goes from left to right. So, processes or actions to the right happen after processes are shown to their left. Each 'lane' of the diagram is used to show the involvement of a specific person or team (Figure 5.2).

Services are designed for people, so it is usual to start with the service user or patient on the top line. This is also useful in helping services to see how much – or how little – of the process is visible to the person using the service, and how much time elapses between their periods of involvement.

The detail of a diagram will depend on the scale of the process being reviewed. So, if looking at an outpatient process from a hospital perspective, having the primary care process as one 'lane' may be fine. If looking at processes within General Practice, using multiple lanes to represent different staff groups may be necessary.

Taking a common outpatient process, a patient may go to see their primary care physician. The patient's experience will occupy the first swim lane, and the primary care physician – a General Practitioner or 'GP' in the UK – will occupy the second lane.

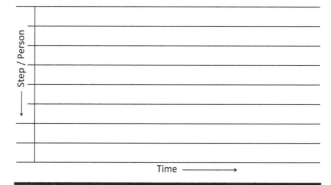

Figure 5.2 Axes of a Swim Lane Diagram

The GP will assess the patient and may make a referral to a secondary care service. That referral will generally go through an appointment process (Lane 3), the patient will receive an appointment (the patient's involvement is shown in Lane 1) and will attend an OP appointment with a specialist (Lane 4). This may lead to more investigations (Lane 5) which will require an appointment (Lane 1) and then a further OP appointment (Lane 4, also shown in Lane 1 as it is a touchpoint with the patient). This may lead to a treatment which requires notification to the GP (Lane 2) who then provides a prescription to a pharmacy (Lane 6) which is collected by the patient (Lane 1).

Figure 5.3 shows a Swim Lane Diagram looking in detail at attendance at an out-patient clinic.

Process with a Team

In working with a team, consider in advance whether you have the right range of people. Staff will often believe they know what other staff members do, but when they are in different roles, they may be wrong. There is also an issue of respect: people do jobs day in and day out. It is unreasonable to assume that a person doing a different job, however senior, knows more about the detail of an individual's job than they do themselves. Consider inviting service user participants to the session.

In the appointment process above, if the focus is on secondary care, it may not be essential to have primary care staff represented, particularly if the focus of the

improvement work – the scope – is going to be on the secondary care process. If the focus was on the initial primary care referral, then a different group of staff would be required.

Assuming the work is focused on secondary care, the mapping is likely to require:

■ The service receiving and triaging referrals, and booking appointments.
■ The service undertaking the assessments.
■ Imaging or investigation-related departments if this is an essential part of the process.
■ A patient who has recently navigated the service themselves could also add valuable insights.

When the group gathers, have a round of introductions. Do not assume that everyone knows one another. It is useful to ask people to introduce themselves with their name, job title and a brief description of their role. If service users are taking part, some job titles may need explanation.

Explain to the team that the purpose of the mapping session is to describe what happens at present, rather than to produce an idealised state or a preferred future state. Let them know that there will be opportunities to design an ideal state later in the process.

Note in advance that you want to map the main route through the service, and that there may be some variation. Explain the concept of the 80/20 rule. Describe the structure of the diagram. Not everyone will tune into this straightaway, but everyone will get the hang of it when the mapping begins.

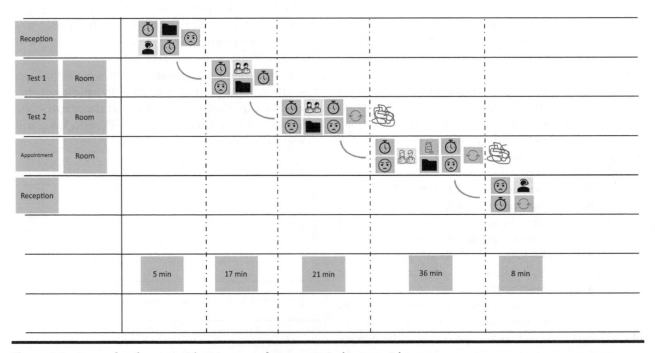

Figure 5.3   Example of an outpatient process shown on a Swim Lane Diagram

Mapping

Start with the patient, on the top line. Write 'Patient' (or the services' preferred term, such as 'Service User' or 'Client') on the note. Use it to label the top line. Very occasionally, you may be mapping an entirely internal process that only has the identity of staff groups, in which case the top line may be different.

Ask the group *'what happens first?'* Tease out how the contact happens (telephone, face to face, etc.) including what technology is required (e.g., a computer with which to e-mail, a tablet to log data), what programmes or forms are needed (e.g., a particular software program, a specific printed form) and exactly who is involved.

You can then use these categories – who; how the contact happens; any required technology and what information vehicles (forms, programmes) are needed – in all the subsequent actions. It is useful to use different coloured sticky notes for the different categories, to make it easier to see what relates to which category. Having a key to the colours used at the side for reference is helpful for participants.

Identify any problems that occur at each step, such as delays, errors or rework, and add them to the diagram. Make it clear to the group that the process is mapping what happens, as opposed to what they would like to happen. Part of the role of the facilitator is to protect staff and allow their voice to be heard, even when they may describe things that others did not know happened and may prefer to deny (see Box 5.1).

This requires constant attention to what people are saying. The advantage of two facilitators is that one can take care of the mechanical aspects – writing notes, putting them up – and the second facilitator can concentrate on the conversation. These roles are not exclusive, and if the person completing the map hears something relevant that the person leading the discussion seems to have missed, they can pick it up directly, or bring it to the attention of the other facilitator.

Summarise

It is very easy for people to get lost in the detail. To avoid this, pause every now and again to summarise the process as described so far. This reminds people that there is a whole process to map and helps to promote a shared understanding. It also gives the group members a chance to bring up any issues they feel have been overlooked, or not accurate. Rather than correcting one another, which can be difficult, they can correct the narrator.

BOX 5.1 COMMON ISSUES IN PROCESS MAPPING AND RESPONSES

1. Overinclusion

Staff often want to capture every eventuality. If multiple options are offered, ask how often each of them happens. Sometimes asking when an option last occurred can identify it as an uncommon situation. Use the 80/20 rule. If staff have difficulty letting go of a previous event, write it down on your 'Parking Lot' sheet, so that people can see it is not being ignored.

2. Describing an ideal state

People often begin by describing the process they think should happen, rather than what does happen. If you hear voices of dissent or you know from observations that what is being described is not realistic, then pull people back to what *does* happen.

3. Denying a problem

Having a group of people discuss a process in detail is an unusual situation. It is unsurprising that staff sometimes feel threatened and even embarrassed if a problem is identified. Sometimes, people try to minimise an issue or deny its existence altogether. They may be right, but often there is a genuine problem. It also denies the experience of others or dismisses the importance of their observation. Remind the group that they are describing the current state; that no one will have designed the whole process; that they want to identify as many issues as possible so they can decide what they want to tackle; and that there is no blame – the group is looking at a process, not the work done by individuals.

Moving through the Process

Be clear about how much time you have, and that there will not be a further session: this is the one chance to get it done. Debating things is interesting, and people may want to go into greater detail on variants than is required. The facilitators must keep things moving. This often requires a mixture of summarising, reminding people that they are looking at the common pathways and that they want to get through the whole process so they can achieve a collective view of what areas of the process they want to prioritise.

Occasionally people come in late and want to unpick much of what has already been done. This is not possible and gives the impression that the views of the person who has arrived late, for whatever reason, are more important or 'more correct' than the collective views of the group who have been working through the rest of the session. Briefly summarising the process to date can be helpful and fits in with the summarising method. If the person has a point, pin them down on how important it is: what proportion of people does it affect, and how big a difference it makes to what has been mapped. Consider whether it makes a material difference or if it is a detail. Often it can be added on a note to satisfy the latecomer, but without delaying the rest of the group unduly. Sometimes one facilitator may need to peel off to speak to the person, to understand the point they are making. Once they understand it, if it is relevant, they can add it to the developing process diagram and comment on it in the next summary.

Protecting Service Users

Service users are giving up their own time to try to help, usually because they want the process to be better for others. The facilitators have an important task of letting their voice be heard, and respecting their views, while also allowing for professional detail. Paraphrasing can be useful to help lay people stay involved and asking staff to explain briefly a technical point will probably be useful for more than the lay person.

Sometimes a lay person wants to spend a great deal of time on one point, usually because they were directly affected by it, or have heard of others who were. As with the time pressures for professional staff, it is important to acknowledge the point and to make it clear that it has been heard, but not to let the session grind to a halt.

Identifying Flow

Towards the end of the session, once you have the process set out, it can be useful to identify flow. This both reminds people of the importance of the concept and restates the importance of the way the steps of the process work together. Ask people which parts of the process flow with no delays and link them with green wool or green tape. Where things can be slow, use yellow wool/tape. Where there are delays of blockages, use red wool/tape. If there is rework, you can identify it with a swirl of red wool/tape. It sounds messy, but it can give a good impression of the overall flow of the process.

Prioritisation

Every time a person raises an idea for improvement, hand them an Ideas Form. Do this conspicuously: after a while people will begin to pick them up as they think of a new idea.

Unless it is a remarkably smooth process, the group will identify a lot of potential improvement targets, and several ideas for ways to tackle the identified problems. Avoid talking about solutions at this stage. It is helpful to ask people not what they would do, but where the big areas of work seem to be. This does not need to be definitive – indeed, without all the data it should be indicative only – but it can be a very helpful support to allow a team to begin to take a view of where the biggest issues might be. Even if these are not the areas that are eventually targeted, once they see other sources of information, the idea that they are going to discuss the process, and decide what to work on, is powerful.

Acknowledging the Work

End the session by running back through the whole process described by the team. This will build on earlier summaries, so need not be onerous. It lets the team hear the summary of their work and helps them to feel that their voice has been heard and their expertise acknowledged. Refer to any issues on the Parking Lot to assure them that they are not forgotten, note the number of ideas generated and link the work to the rest of the improvement event. Thank them for their effort. Above all, be respectful of people's time and expertise.

Conclusions

Process mapping with a team is a powerful process. It lets people see the whole process, sometimes for the first time. It allows everyone present to see how their part of the work fits with the wider process. Because it is a communal activity, no role is taken to be more important than another, which is a compelling message for staff who may not all be used to being listened to with respect and interest within their hierarchy. The visual layout works for many people, and it is of great value when creating the Value Stream Map. It is also very useful within the RPIW.

Chapter 6

Planning Meetings

Introduction

The purpose of the planning meetings is to keep the RPIW on track. RPIWs are expensive events, and it is essential to be fully prepared. Twelve people attending an RPIW for a week is the equivalent of one person working full time for three months. It is better to delay or cancel an RPIW than to use the time unwisely.

Scheduling in four planning meetings works well: it is possible to cancel a meeting if the work is going particularly well and it is not needed but scheduling them to ensure people are available is sensible. This chapter assumes there are four planning meetings and spreads the work accordingly: if a different number of meetings is used, then the schedule can be adapted accordingly. At least a week is needed between planning meetings to allow agreed work to be undertaken. The form shown in Figure 3.3 can be used to keep track of meeting dates.

The Process Owner and at least one of the facilitators must be present at each meeting. Ideally, both facilitators should attend all planning meetings so that they are fully briefed. The stages to be undertaken at each planning meeting are included below so that they can be consulted before a meeting. This results in some repetition in the text but helps to avoid anything being overlooked.

Planning Meeting One

Value Stream Map

Share the current version of the Value Stream Map (Figures 4.15 and 4.16). At a minimum, this must have the process steps. Timings, Work in Process and other metrics can be collected as part of the agreed measurement plan (see

---

below). Use the current state of the Value Stream Map to agree on the focus of the RPIW.

Discuss what additional data needs to be collected and agree on an observation plan. This may need to be amended as more details are gathered, but a basic plan is needed to get started and to prioritise observations. Discuss the likely metrics and agree on how any relevant work will be commissioned, such as analysis of databases or other secondary data sources.

Agree with the customer for the process and discuss how customer/patient/client views will be collected and analysed.

Project Form

Discuss who will be in the Away Team and who is needed for the Advisory Group (Figure 3.1). It is important that every staff group who may be affected by the results is represented in the Away Team. A reasonable number of

---

participants is 8–10 and anything over 12 participants is likely to be too large for a single RPIW.

This is a good time to agree on how patient participants will be identified and recruited. This may take some time, so it is important to begin work on identifying patient representatives at this first meeting.

Preparing the People

The facilitators and the Process Owner must ensure that Away Team members clear their diaries for the event. The Process Owner will be able to do this for people in their direct line management span, but the facilitators will need to liaise with the line managers of other staff to ensure that they are available.

The extent to which the Home Team, the remaining members of the service, are involved should be reviewed. Check what they know and understand of the RPIW and its aims. Agree on how to brief them, and who will do this. See Chapter 4 for further discussion of staff briefings and how staff can be updated as the work progresses.

Share and Spread

Discuss what areas may learn from the current work. If there are areas where it may be relevant to adopt the work, consider how to link the teams from these additional settings. A plan will often be needed so that they are aware of the work.

In some cases, it makes sense to involve staff who work in adjacent processes. For example, working in an acute admission ward may need involvement from the Emergency Department or from a Discharge Support Team. If appropriate, a member can be invited onto the Away Team for the event.

In other cases, there may be a similar service in a different location which could learn from the work. Again, consider whether a representative should join the RPIW, or whether attendance at the Report Out may be adequate.

Confirm the time, date and location of Planning Meeting Two.

Planning Meeting Two

Both the Process Owner and the Sponsor should be present. As before, a facilitator can chair the meeting and the meeting should be no longer than an hour. Longer meetings are often a warning sign that there is an unidentified problem, or time is not being identified for sufficient work between meetings.

Value Stream Map

Review the Value Stream Map. It should now be close to complete, including the timings of steps and the volume of Work in Process at each step should be identified. Agree on what else needs to be collected, and how this will be done, and by whom. Takt time should be known for this meeting, and the information can be shared and discussed.

Project Form

It is helpful to discuss the scope and direction of the work and to check that the information being collected is relevant to the aims. Look again at the boundaries of the process agreed upon in the first meeting and confirm that these still make sense in the light of observations and further data obtained since then. It may be better to have a more focused RPIW if it has become clear that there is a great deal of work to do. In other cases, observations may suggest that a referral process is also key, for example, and should be included.

Review the Away Team membership and check that everyone required is listed. Observations may have identified an additional role that needs to be represented, or changes to scope may mean that a person previously expected to take part is no longer required. Confirm that all Away Team and Advisory Group members have been contacted for their availability. Check what progress has been made on patient representation and agree whether additional work is required to identify a person or persons for this role.

Pre-Event Work

As discussed in Chapter 5, it is very helpful to conduct process mapping with the wider team, both to promote engagement and to ensure that as wide a group as possible can input their views. Agree on when this will be done, and how a wider group can be involved.

Preparing the People

Check how Home Team engagement is progressing, discuss any concerns and agree on how to address them. If a Waste Wheel has not already been put up, agree on when this will be done. It can be usefully linked to staff briefings so that people are clear on its purpose. Ideas Forms should also be discussed, although they may not be distributed until later in the process (Figure 4.14).

Target Metric Report

Discuss targets and check that they align with the focus of the RPIW. Consider what targets can reasonably be addressed in the RPIW, and how they will be measured. The Sponsor should advise on the size of expected improvements, such as percentage reduction or improvement. An example of a Target Metric Report is shown in Figure 6.1.

Target Metric Report (TMR)
Sheet 1 - RPIW Outputs

	Team Name		
	Department		
	Product / Process Summary		

	Date of Improvement Event		TO
	Process Owner		Executive Sponsor
	Improvement Lead 1		Takt Time
	Improvement Lead 2		

	Metric (Unit of Measurement) & Narrative	Baseline	Target	Day 2	Day 3	Day 4	Final	% Change against Baseline
1	Efficiency Gain							
	%							
2	Inventory							
	£s							
3	Quality							
	%							
4	Quality							
	%							
5	5S							
	Levels 1 to 4							
	Additional Comments							

HQIS 2022
Version 1.01

Figure 6.1 Target Metric Report

Confirm the time, date and location of Planning Meeting Three

Planning Meeting Three

By this stage, the Value Stream Map should be complete (Figures 4.15 and 4.16). The Project Form should also be finalised at this meeting (Figure 3.1). This includes a final list of the Away Team and Advisory Group, and confirmation that the people have agreed attendance. It is important to check what support has been agreed for the patient representative(s) and who is providing it.

Preparing the People

Discuss the process mapping exercise and share any feedback from it. Review the progress of the Waste Wheel/Wheels. If Ideas Forms have not already been issued, agree on how it will be done. If it has already started, take a few minutes to review the range of ideas that have been suggested. This can be useful in beginning to think through possible work streams. Agree on who will send joining instructions to the Away Team, and check that the Advisory Group has received an update. If they have not been updated, agree on who will take on this task.

Target Progress Report

This should be very close to its final version. Discuss any outstanding data collection. Review what patient/client experience data has been obtained and whether any further work is required to ensure it is available for the RPIW week. Figure 6.2 shows an example with baseline and targets included.

Post-Event Activity

This is a good time to discuss work after the event. The facilitators should talk over post-RPIW work with the Process Owner, including the importance of measurement. Most systems have updates, for example, at one month, three months and six months. Discuss how data will be obtained to look at progress.

Confirm the time and location of Planning Meeting Four.

Planning Meeting Four

Planning Meeting Four should ideally be a relaxed affair, with most or all the preparatory work already completed.

If not, it is essential to complete the final preparations at this meeting.

Review Standard Documentation

Take the time to run over the standard documentation including the Value Stream Map (Figures 4.15 and 4.16), Work Combination Record (Figures 4.9 and 4.10), Process Work Sheet (Figures 4.7 and 4.8) and the takt time calculation (Figures 2.1 and 4.3). It is important that the Process Owner and Sponsor understand what they show.

Target Progress Report

Finalise the Target Progress Report (Figure 6.2) if this has not already been done. The Sponsor should confirm their agreement with the targets. Take the opportunity to check that the Process Owner knows how all the measurements have been obtained and knows how to repeat them after the RPIW. If not, a facilitator should meet with the Process Owner as it is important that the Process Owner is comfortable with measurement and the details of the agreed metrics to avoid causing them unnecessary pressure or confusion after the event.

RPIW Plans

Confirm that joining details have been sent to the Away Team, with details of the venue, timings, etc.

Ensure that the Sponsor knows the location and time, and when they are expected to attend. This includes attending for an introduction on Day One and for briefings on Days Two and Three. Check that they have also set time aside to attend the Report Out.

Take a few moments to check if there are any final issues or concerns. It is much better to identify them at this point than at the RPIW itself as there is still time to act on any new issues.

Post-Event Activity

Discuss the Process Owner's responsibilities after the RPIW and talk about any support that they may require. Check that there is a plan for any identified spread and share opportunities.

Conclusions

Different organisations will vary in their planning meeting processes. This chapter sets out one possible approach. The learning is that careful preparation is required. RPIWs are

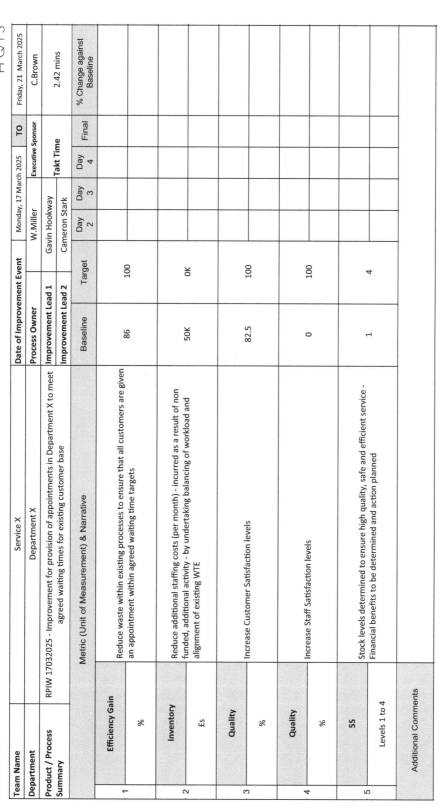

Target Metric Report (TMR)
Sheet 1 - RPIW Outputs

Team Name	Service X	Date of Improvement Event		Monday, 17 March 2025	TO	Friday, 21 March 2025
Department	Department X	Process Owner		W.Miller	Executive Sponsor	C.Brown
Product / Process Summary	RPIW 17032025 - Improvement for provision of appointments in Department X to meet agreed waiting times for existing customer base	Improvement Lead 1		Gavin Hookway	**Takt Time**	2.42 mins
		Improvement Lead 2		Cameron Stark		

	Metric (Unit of Measurement) & Narrative	Baseline	Target	Day 2	Day 3	Day 4	Final	% Change against Baseline
1	**Efficiency Gain** % Reduce waste within existing processes to ensure that all customers are given an appointment within agreed waiting time targets	86	100					
2	**Inventory** £s Reduce additional staffing costs (per month) - incurred as a result of non funded, additional activity - by undertaking balancing of workload and alignment of existing WTE	50K	0K					
3	**Quality** % Increase Customer Satisfaction levels	82.5	100					
4	**Quality** % Increase Staff Satisfaction levels	0	100					
5	**5S** Levels 1 to 4 Stock levels determined to ensure high quality, safe and efficient service - Financial benefits to be determined and action planned	1	4					
	Additional Comments							

HQIS 2022
Version 1.01

Figure 6.2   Example of Target Metric Report with baseline and targets

expensive and time-consuming events, and it is essential that the organisation does everything it can to ensure that they will have as much value as possible.

The Sponsor plays a pivotal role in making links to organisational strategy, helping with any problems that arise and setting targets. The Process Owner may be new to RPIWs and can require considerable support. Engagement of the Home Team is very important and, together with patient involvement, should be a core part of the preparation.

Chapter 7

RPIW, Day Minus One

Final Check on Event

It is sensible to do a final check with the Sponsor to make sure they understand that they are needed for the first part of the following Monday morning. In some large organisations, checking with their Personal Assistant that they have it in their diary, and that it clearly states the location and time, may be as much as you can do. If you have their mobile number, consider texting the Sponsor a message saying that you are looking forward to their input on Monday. At worst, this acts as a reminder that they are due to come along.

It is also worth checking for any last-minute apologies for the event. This is uncommon but does occur from time to time. This can happen because of illness, an unexpected carer responsibility, or sometimes because of a problem in a clinical team. It may be too late to make any changes, but it does allow you to consider whether additional support may be needed during the week. For example, if a person in a specific profession drops out, if you cannot replace them, you will usually be able to arrange to check in with a person in that specialty or profession several times during the week.

If there is a service user representative, it can be useful to call them to check if they have any last-minute questions about the event. This also allows you to confirm that they know the location of the event, and how to get there.

Information on the Room

Remind yourself of the rules around the room. Can you move furniture? What can you use to attach things to walls? In some rooms, adhesive putty is allowed, but not tape, in others both are permitted. Checking in advance reduces the scope for unintended conflict, and for later bills for re-decoration if paint is damaged.

There will be standard information on fire exits, toilet locations and planned fire alarms. Checking this in advance of the event, and keeping the information handy, is very useful to save having to look for it on Day One.

If you are providing teas or coffees, check when they are due to arrive and whether the trolley will be left outside the room, or will be brought inside. If it is to be brought inside, check whether you can bring in the trolley without moving participants. It is better to adjust the room in advance to avoid moving people during the event.

Check the arrangements for cleaning the room. Some venues expect access for cleaners at a specific time, when there may still be participants in the room. It is worth considering whether you want cleaners to enter the room at all. You may prefer to not have cleaners access the room during the event, and if so, this must be agreed upon with the relevant supervisor. If that is the case, time must be included to have a quick tidying of the room at the end of each day.

In other instances, cleaning may be useful, but you may want tables, charts and papers to be left where they are. Again, this should be arranged in advance with the facilities manager or housekeeping supervisor. As with most things in Lean, speaking to the people involved directly to explain the purpose of the event, how you expect it to flow and why specific arrangements are helpful to you, is better than a directive. The housekeeping staff will often have good ideas about how to work around the event and how to support it once they understand the process.

Occasionally, an event is run in a room which will be used for other purposes in the evening. This greatly adds to the work of the coordinators. It is best to explain the problem to the team, who will usually help you to clear away the material at the end of the day. Setting up in the morning in this situation usually falls to the Workshop Lead and Team Lead and it cuts into preparation time. Avoid a shared room if possible.

DOI: 10.4324/9780429020742-7

Preparing the Room

RPIWs happen in spaces of many sizes and shapes. Some organisations have custom-made facilities, but in most cases, teams use either generic training rooms or meeting rooms. Inevitably, these are different shapes and layouts, and the workshop leaders need to adapt to this.

It can be necessary to set up on the day because you cannot obtain access in advance. More often, as RPIWs usually start on a Monday at the start of the working week, it is possible to get into the room after the last meeting on the previous Friday. This may be the last thing the workshop leads want to do after a busy week, but it can make a big difference when Monday morning comes around.

Whether you are setting up in advance, or doing it at 7 am on a Monday morning, assess the room. Check where you can project an image and look for the location of the power points. Ensure that cables reach from power points to your equipment. Identify the largest areas of blank walls that can be used for mapping and for displaying information.

will help in some of the training exercises on Day One. It also helps to avoid people feeling that it is difficult to stand and move around, which can be constraining for some of the later exercises. If relevant, think about wheelchair access.

In an RPIW, it is helpful to encourage people to move around the room early in the first session. RPIWs are a participation sport and messaging as early as possible that the team will not spend the whole event sitting at tables is valuable. The Data Wall (see below) is reviewed on Day One, and it is useful to set it up in a location where the team must stand up and move to see it. This is not always possible but is worth doing if you can.

Place a Flip Chart stand with Flip Chart at a convenient location in the room, where you can reach it without walking behind sitting participants, if possible. See Figure 7.1 for an example.

Keep in mind sensible safety precautions. Tape down any loose power leads or other cables. Carry appropriate tape in your kit for this purpose: there are many other uses for it.

Room Arrangement

The commonest set-up for Day One is to arrange a table to allow participants to see the screen and to be able to take notes. A U-shaped arrangement often works well (Figure 7.1) with a table arranged to hold the projector and computer being used to run presentations. In some rooms, you may have a separate dais wired for the presentation equipment.

When arranging the seats and tables, try to leave sufficient space for people to move behind the seats, as this

Signposting the Room

The joining instructions sent out to the team include information on the location. Health and social care environments can still be complex, and helpful notices showing the route on the day can avoid delays and confusion. Walk back to the entrance and look for where there are route choices. You may wish to add a temporary notice at these locations. In some cases, where there are access-controlled doors, it may be necessary to have a team member wait

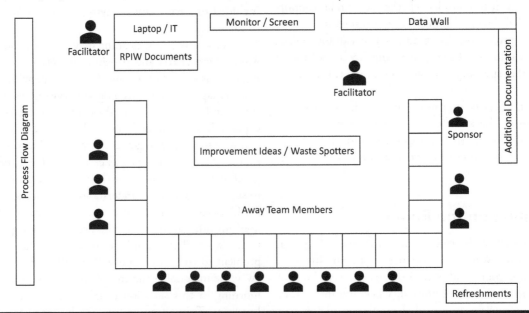

Figure 7.1　Possible room arrangement

at the door on the first morning to make sure people can gain access.

If you do not want participants to enter the room until you have completed setting up, then add a printed sheet to the outside of the door, with text such as

'(insert title) RPIW / Room Set Up Underway / Please do not Enter until 8.50am').

Items for the Walls

Items can be placed on the walls in readiness. These will usually be a sheet of Flip Chart paper. Their purpose is discussed further in the 'Day One' chapter and they include:

- A 'Ground Rules' sheet
- A 'Feelings'
- An 'Expectations' Sheet
- A Smiley Face sheet – usually three columns with a smiley face, a neutral face and a sad face
- The Waste Wheel collated during the run-up to the event

Putting these up in advance helps the flow of the event and reduces the need to scurry around during the session.

Data Wall

Getting the Data Wall right can help to get the work off to a good start. The purpose of a Data Wall is to tell a story and to provide both information to get people started, and reference material that can be consulted and used during the event.

When setting it out, think of the narrative. Work out the story that is being conveyed.

Different organisations have different norms for what goes on to a Data Wall, but you cannot go far wrong if you keep in mind the need to tell a compelling story that helps people to unite to resolve a quality problem.

One possible sequence of information is:

1. The Project Form / A3 for the work
2. The targets for the work, compared to current performance, often using a Target Metrics Report or similar
3. Information on the process, such as:
   a. Completed Direct Observation Records
   b. Work Combination Record
   c. Work Balance Chart
   d. Takt time calculation

4. Graphs, photographs and tables relevant to the process
5. Any useful documents and existing Standard Work
6. Current State Value Stream Map

BOX 7.1 PRACTICE TIP: PREPARING A DATA WALL

Data walls can be challenging to get right. If you put the documents in individual, clear plastic folders, it is easy to handle them and to try different combinations until you can develop a sequence of presentation that helps to tell the story of the information gathered in advance of the event.

It is easiest to do this on a long table or a spare section of the floor. Ask yourself the story you are trying to tell. Some of the Away Team will be well acquainted with the data, but no matter how much work you put into communication in advance of the event, there will be other people who have given it little or no thought until the event. Even if you have met everyone, not everyone will remember all you discussed.

Don't attempt to tape the plastic folders down until you are happy that the order explains the important issues and will support the introductory session.

It takes time to do this, so once you have an order that works, tape them onto a long piece of paper, such as a paper roll. Tape the top and bottom edge of the plastic pocket onto the paper in the order you have decided, leaving the short edge open to allow you to extract the paper if required. If it is a vertical form or sheet, tape the long edges, leaving the top free to extract the sheet.

If you carefully roll up the whole roll, it is easier to move it to its eventual location. Unrolling it and taping it to a wall can be tricky. Two people can manage it and three should be able to place the roll on the wall with reasonable ease.

Equipment for the RPIW

Momentum is important in an RPIW. Ideally, all required kit should be there when people need it. It is not possible to account for every possible eventuality, but experience shows that many items are needed time and time again. The precise list will depend on the technology used in the host organisation. Networked printers, built in audio-visual equipment, strength of wireless network connections and the software preferred by an organisation will all affect the final requirements.

In the North of Scotland where much of our practice has been undertaken, network connections, wireless signals and Bluetooth strength – even cell phone signals – are often suspect. Our belt and braces recommended core kit for a standalone event with minimal organisational infrastructure includes:

Audio-visual
    Projector, with cable to link to computer
    Laptop computer with required presentations, required forms and printer driver pre-installed
    Portable printer, with cable to link to computer
    Visualiser
    Power cable: a cable reel can be useful
    Spare ink cartridges for printer
Office supplies
    Sheaf of A4 paper, or local equivalent
    Scissors
    Lead pencils
    Coloured pencils
    Pens
    Stapler
    Whiteboard pens, several colours
    Indelible markers
    Hole punch
    Laminator, and plastic pockets for laminator
    Packet of punched plastic folders
    Masking tape
    Sellotape or equivalent
    At least one roll of Flip Chart paper
    Sticky notes – multiple pads of different colours
    Large sticky notes – several colours
    Adhesive putty
Exercises
    Supplies for any exercises you have chosen for Day One

Food and Drink

Infection control requirements are important to follow. Commonly during a major community outbreak, the organisation will not want any shared arrangements and the team will have to adapt accordingly.

If shared facilities are acceptable at the time of the RPIW, if you are not having tea and coffee delivered, decide if you are going to make it available. If so, you will need a kettle, access to a water supply, cups, sugar, sweeteners, milk (different types as required), spoons and a bin.

Think about how you lay it out for easy use: it is a Lean event, after all.

Many facilitators place small baskets of sweets and/or fruit on the tables, for use by the participants. Some facilitators, if they have the appropriate skills, bake for the event and take cakes or other bakes to the event. This kind of personal effort is usually appreciated, and you often find that others reciprocate and bring in food they have prepared. Some common sense is needed. Don't let people bring in homemade coleslaw and leave it in a warm room until lunchtime, for example. Think about allergies. If you have a participant with a severe nut allergy, for example, you may not be able to have any food in the room and may need to let other participants know in advance so that they can avoid bringing in anything that could cause the person problems.

Homemade cakes and breads are generally fine unless your organisation has a health and safety policy that precludes it. Don't force it. If it happens, it happens. If not, it's not a sign of a problem with the event. It depends on the mix of people, how well they know one another and what their specific interests might be. We worked in an organisation where the Chief Executive and the Head of HR both baked and often brought in baked goods, which had a trickle-down effect on others. Other organisations just don't do it. Either is fine.

Final Check

Do a survey of the room. Check that it looks the way you want.

Put your 'Welcome to the RPIW' sign on the door. As discussed earlier, if you decided on a 'Please do not enter before 8 am', or whatever time is appropriate sign, you can add it. The reason for doing this is to let the facilitators do a last check in the morning to make sure janitorial staff have not rearranged the room or similar spanner in the works.

Leave a sign asking the janitorial staff not to rearrange the room over the evening/weekend in case there has been a communication problem.

On the way out, check the access to the room. Add any temporary signs that may be needed to get people to the right place the following morning or after the weekend depending on when you are setting up. You will need to check them again on Monday morning so take spares in case they have been taken down over the weekend.

Chapter 8

Day One

Introduction

Day One sets the tone for the whole event. Both facilitators and the Process Owner need to be present for the whole day and to be ready to confer and to act as required. A possible agenda with timings is shown in Table 8.1. This shows a Day One structure that the book authors have used in over 100 RPIWs. Different organisations and facilitators will teach techniques most useful to their processes and to how their teams are structured. People using the book to plan an RPIW should feel free to adapt it to suit their workflow.

Get there early. If the event starts at 9 am, arriving at 7.30 am is reasonable if you were not able to set up the previous evening in as much detail as you wanted. Check the room is as you left it and make any final changes. Check with the Process Owner, who should also arrive promptly, if they are aware of any last-minute changes, such as staff illness or a domestic emergency. Check the laptop and projector are working and are on the slide set you want to use. Once you are ready, remove any signs asking people not to enter the room.

As people arrive, the facilitators should introduce themselves. This is a good opportunity to chat and to get to know people. Some participants will know one another, but probably not all. In some large services, not everyone who works in the same area will know one another, particularly if they work on different shifts. Keep an eye out for people who seem to be excluded from the group chat and include them. This can also occur when people are attending who work in processes, such as administration, supplies and laboratories, or are from neighbouring services. This is an early opportunity to model the inclusive behaviour that is essential in RPIWs to gain maximum benefit from everyone's experience and to give all participants a positive experience.

When the Sponsor arrives, check that they have what they need, and remind them of their Day Two and Day Three meetings, and the arrangements for the Report Out on Day Five. The Sponsor should introduce themselves to the participants. The participants need to be confident that the Sponsor will help them as required and has a genuine interest in their service and in their views, experience and ideas. Informal conversations when the participants can see respectful attention from the Sponsor can go a long way towards reducing the perceived distance from the more senior person.

Getting Started

Start promptly at 9.00 am or any other agreed start time. Sticking to time is important and gives a message for the rest of the week. If anyone is not there, start anyway.

Each facilitator will have a slightly different approach, but a common structure would be:

- A brief introduction from one of the facilitators, welcoming people to the event. This can include the usual details such as information on fire exits, planned fire drills and location of toilets.
- A round of introductions – usually name, job title and what they hope to get from the event.
- The Sponsor's welcome.
- An icebreaker.
- What participants feel about the event.
- What they hope the outcome of the event will be.
- Agreement of ground rules.

The purpose of these opening actions is to give everyone a chance to speak, no matter what their usual role, to give the feeling that this may be different from other workshops, to identify any worries or concerns, and to have notice of what people want to achieve, which may not always be what the Sponsor and Process Owner want from the event.

DOI: 10.4324/9780429020742-8

Table 8.1 Example of a Day One Agenda

0900	Welcome and Housekeeping Introductions
0910	Sponsor's Welcome
0920	Overview of the Week Fears and Expectations of Participants House Rules The RPIW Process The Teams What Is an RPIW? RPIW Roles
0945	Data Wall Walk – Review Project Form/Target Metric Form/Value Stream Map
1000	Value and Waste Ideas Generation
1020	Break
1035	5S & Exercise Ideas Generation
1120	Visual Control and Kanban Ideas Generation
1140	Error-Proofing Ideas Generation
1210	Set-Up Reduction & Exercise Ideas Generation
1240	Lunchbreak
1315	Improvement Cycles Ideas Generation
1335	Standard Work Ideas Generation
1405	Continuous Flow Ideas Generation
1450	Break
1500	Practical Exercise Ideas Generation
1600	Review of Current State Ideas Generation
1645	Plans for the Rest of the Week/Evaluations
1700	Close of Day One

If there are patient, carer or advocacy group participants, this is a good opportunity to show the behaviours expected towards them. The facilitators can treat them like all other members of the team. Staff members are generally familiar with introducing themselves in a workgroup, but it is useful in the earlier meetings with patient/carer participants to tell them that there will be a round of introductions so that they are prepared.

Sponsor's Introduction

The Sponsor may have to speak before the Feelings and Expectations exercise, but if they can stay for the exercise, they can be slotted in to speak afterwards. Speaking after the Feelings and Expectations exercise is preferable as it lets them hear concerns and hopes and demonstrates that they are willing to devote time to the event. Most of the people who act as Sponsors will be sufficiently used to thinking on their feet to incorporate ideas from the introductions and exercises into their briefing.

The Sponsor's task is to put the work of the week in context. They can explain why it has been chosen, why it is important and how it fits into the overall work of the organisation. The tone of this presentation is important. It should not sound as if the senior management team feel the people working in the service have failed and are being picked out for remedial attention. They

---

BOX 8.1 PRACTICE TIP – FEELINGS AND EXPECTATIONS

The easiest way to obtain this is to give each participant two differently coloured sticky notes. Use the same colours for all participants. Have two flip chart sheets in the wall, one marked 'Feelings' and one marked 'Expectations'.

Explain that one colour – yellow, say – is for their Feelings about the event, and that the other colour is for their Expectations – what they want from the event. Writing the colours and questions on a whiteboard is useful and reduces confusion. Sticking the relevant colour of a sticky note beside the question is a simple visual cue.

Some people will want to write down more than one thing, so scatter a supply of sticky notes of the appropriate colours on the desktops. Have more in reserve in case they are required. Encourage everyone to commit by completing at least one sticky note of each colour.

Ask the group to put their sticky notes on the relevant sheet. This begins to give a chance for people to leave their seat. Now and again a room is so small as to make this difficult but try to get people out of their seats as often as possible. They are active participants, and they need to feel like participants rather than passive observers attending a seminar.

One facilitator can read out the list once people have stopped adding new notes. The other facilitator should listen for themes, and for any issues that seem to be implicit but are not picked up by the first facilitator. Either facilitator can group them into themes, with the other helping.

On Feelings, a typical range includes anxiety, uncertainty, hopefulness, enthusiasm for learning new methods and interest. Sometimes people will express frustration – *'we should have agreed this already'*; concern, *'I'm worried that we take a whole week out and that nothing gets better'*, or even anger, *'annoyed that we are wasting time on this when we have so much to do'*. It is important to acknowledge any concerns, including feelings of guilt that others are continuing with their normal job while this group is being given time out.

The facilitators do not need to have an answer for everything, nor to understand all the points being made the first time. No one has complete knowledge, and it is not necessary to pretend otherwise. If the facilitator is not sure what a point means, they can ask for clarification. Often the person who wrote it will expand on the point they made.

It is straightforward to give some reassurance about being away from work: the group will be working hard and will check out all their ideas with the Home Team, the people still working in the area. The pressures that make staff feel guilty about taking time to attend an improvement workshop are usually the reasons the work is being done. The event allows the group to produce and test ideas for ways to better serve their patient/client group.

On the concern that nothing will change, the facilitators can remind the group of the organisational commitment, including the involvement of the Sponsor. It is useful to note that there will be regular reports on progress after the event and chances to revisit the actions to make sure that they are delivering the hoped-for improvement.

In response to annoyance that things have not already been settled, the facilitators can observe that, if it were straightforward, it would already have been done. The ongoing challenges are the reason for the organisation investing this time in an event.

On Expectations, common responses from the team members are that they hope things will be better after the event; that they will have had an opportunity to work out what to do; that their workload will be more manageable; and that some aspects of quality will have improved. From time to time, someone will write that they expect no improvement to result from the event. Others may well be thinking the same but be unwilling to say it, so this is a useful concern to have in the open.

The facilitators can point out that the organisation is investing considerable resources in the event and its preparation. They can use the chance to make the role of the team clear: that changes are not being developed or imposed by an external group, but rather that the group is being given the opportunity to develop their own solutions for the service they deliver, and in some cases use. The Sponsor can reinforce their commitment to the work. Again, it is not necessary to have an answer to every concern but modelling a willingness to listen and to learn goes a long way to generating goodwill.

can recognise that the people present did not design the current service: very often, no one at all designed the service as it currently exists, and changes have accumulated over time, sometimes moving a service far from what would have been intended when it was established. The Sponsor should be clear that the purpose of the work is to give the service staff the opportunity to step back and to look at the processes they have been asked to use and to redesign them to meet the needs of their clients as well as they can.

This is also an opportunity to be clear that the purpose of the event is not to ladle impossible amounts of work on already busy people. Lean, applied well, includes respect for staff and promotes active engagement and involvement in decision-making. Balancing capacity and demand is important, and recognising that staff may already feel stretched and even overworked is not an admission of failure, but rather a recognition of the human elements of change. By removing waste and rework more can be achieved with less stress.

The Sponsor should be explicit about resource constraints. There is often no new money to be invested in a service, or at least not straight away. Rather than throwing money at a problem, usually by doing more of what has already been found not to work, the purpose of the RPIW is to look at fit with patient/client need and to remove waste and improve flow. This usually results in improvements to patient and staff experience without additional investment. If changes are designed and implemented, and there is still a gap, then the information and experience accumulated mean that any future investment is more likely to meet the true needs of the service, with a redesigned service model. Making constraints explicit is helpful as it helps to avoid people feeling let down later.

The interest of the Sponsor should be clear. They can make a personal undertaking to try to resolve issues escalated to them and confirm that they will stay involved during the following year, take an interest in the project and attend Report Outs.

The Sponsor's intervention can be very powerful. In very large organisations, many staff will not know all, or even any, Directors. Being able to speak to a director in person, and being told that the organisation wants them to develop a revised system for their work and will support them to deliver it, can be very powerful.

Sponsors are usually happy to take questions and should be honest and open in their replies. Sponsors often get a lot out of the interactions in an RPIW week, and often end the week with a much better understanding of the pressures on staff and on the detail of at least one part of the service.

Agreeing Ground Rules

Ground rules can be very valuable. They need to be agreed upon rather than imposed, or people will feel less obligation to stick to them. After expectations and hopes for the event are considered, it is a natural place to say, *'and what ground rules do you want to agree to make sure we get as much out of the week as possible?'*

Writing the points up on a flip chart works well, and the page or pages can then be torn off and mounted on a wall in a prominent position so that they can be consulted during the week. In many organisations, people are used to the idea of setting ground rules, and in some cases, there will be well-understood organisational norms that people can articulate. In some instances, the members will have less experience in setting ground rules. There may also be a range of experience, with some senior staff being familiar with the idea, but newer or more junior staff having less experience. If this proves to be the case, it is important to take some time to make sure that everyone has a chance to contribute, not just those who have gone through the process before.

Common suggestions include:

■ Listen to one another
■ Say what you are thinking
■ No idea is a bad idea
■ Stick to time (often applied to the facilitators as well as the participants)

Facilitators may need to add suggestions that fit with Lean work, such as every person's opinion mattering, and being respectful of the opinions of others. The list created can be very useful, as later in the event it gives participants, or the facilitators, the option to point out the list and remind people that *'we agreed at the start that we were going to listen to everyone/keep to time'*, or whatever the relevant point may be. This reinforces the need for agreement, rather than imposition, if it is to have an impact later.

The approach the facilitators take to the RPIW is very important and affects the likelihood of success. Box 8.2 includes suggestions for the approach facilitators can take.

Project Form

It is worth spending ten minutes or so on the Project Form (Figures 3.1 and 3.2). Some groups of staff will be very familiar with the layout, but others will be new to it. Explaining the scope of the work, the initial observations and the targets helps to set the rest of the work in context. This will be enhanced by the Data Walk.

BOX 8.2   PRACTICE TIP – BEING PRESENT

In many organisations, things happen *to* staff. Decisions are made and passed down to them. People can feel they have no control over their working lives, sometimes resulting in small acts of rebellion.

Lean seeks to put staff front and centre. It encourages staff to reflect on their jobs and the purpose of the service they provide, and to take active steps to improve how it is delivered.

The facilitators at a workshop have an important role in making it clear that this is more than words. There are skills they can apply to make the experience more rewarding for participants, and to demonstrate that their insights and actions are the centre of the process.

Room to speak: In Lean, collective knowledge and ideas are essential, and supporting people to deliver their best efforts is key. When people speak, it must be clear that their input is welcomed, and that their views matter. This may require the facilitators to actively create space for the person to be heard, for example by asking people who talk over others to wait for the other person to finish, and by drawing attention to people who are trying to be heard.

It is also worth being alert to contradictions. In a workshop facilitated by one of the authors, agreements in the session seemed to change rapidly for no apparent reason. Some gentle enquiry revealed that a senior staff member, who was notably quiet in the group sessions, was corralling more junior staff during breaks and telling them to revise their views. This type of behaviour must be made explicit, or the facilitators would both end up running a workshop with an unseen parallel workshop and implicitly endorsing unacceptable behaviour that conflicts with the ethos of Lean.

Active listening: When we listen to people, we are often thinking about what we are going to say, while waiting for others to finish. Facilitators need to do this to some extent, as they will think about how to link a point to previous points, and to note relevant methods that could be applied. Accepting this, the focus needs to be on the point that is being made. The person making the point works in the service, or uses the service, and what they say matters. Paying attention to the point being made is important or the benefits of hard-earned experience can be lost. This needs the facilitators to pay careful attention to all points being made, and to actively encourage others in the group to do so. Some of this can be modelling of behaviour: if the facilitators show careful attention to comments and interventions, others will tend to do so as well. In some instances, it may require a comment, such as '*can we listen to this point, please?*' People may need to be reminded not to talk over one another. Getting this right early on helps to set the tone for the whole RPIW, and to reassure staff that the facilitators are serious about helping their voice to be heard.

Data Walk

The facilitators should take the group through the information collected during the planning phase. The layout of a data wall was discussed in the previous chapter.

Some Process Owners prefer to do the walk-through themselves. This is good but it is also acceptable for a facilitator to tell the story, and to bring in the Process Owner from time to time to illustrate or to expand on points.

The purpose of the Data Walk is to:

■ Demonstrate that there has been a concerted effort to obtain information on the service and its working.
■ Show the issues numerically, and so turn what may have been vague feelings into definite evidence.
■ Give information from different perspectives – demand, user views, timings, waiting lists and capacity.
■ Begin to turn very personally felt work-related pressures into a system problem that can be analysed and considered without it having to be taken as a personal reproach.

■ Give evidence that there is information the workshop participants can use and to which they can compare their changes.

Bringing the voice of the service user into the meeting is important. This is especially so if it has not been possible to secure the participation of service users, carers or a relevant advocacy group. Making sure that user views are represented in the Data Walk is essential and they should be given equal prominence with other types of data.

People may challenge the data. Our experience is that it is uncommon for workshop participants to identify a flaw in the data, particularly as it will have been shared with staff groups during the preparation phase. More often, there is a misunderstanding about numbers or people recall major incidents in the past which have come to dominate their thinking. For example, a clinical team may feel that patients in a particular group are very common, perhaps because of the complexity of care or an adverse incident of some type. Seeing the true numbers can help to counter myths or distortions that have developed over time. Days or weeks with very high numbers of patient referrals stick in people's minds but may not be typical.

It is necessary to be humble: there could be an error in the data and if there is a continuing challenge after an explanation, it is appropriate to offer to check it out and to report back later in the day or week. Generally, the data is confirmed when this is done but it allows people to feel their concerns are being heard and respected. If a mistake is identified, be honest. Acknowledge the error, correct it and thank the person for the intervention.

There can be emotional reactions to the Data Walk. People often do not realise quite how long people are waiting or may not be aware of quality problems. Seeing the number of people being referred for a service may make people feel helpless. The facilitators should acknowledge any concerns or upset. Emphasise that the reason for the work is to improve the situation, and that the organisation is committed to supporting change. The staff are not being abandoned to fix things without support.

Coffee Breaks

Breaks and lunches are important. RPIWs are work, not a retreat, so these breaks are not extendable. Chapter 7 noted that adjustments may be needed for infection control reasons, and in some situations, people may not be able to break into one large group. Whatever the arrangements, try to make breaks run as smoothly as possible by laying items out appropriately. The organisation can usually provide tea, coffee, milk, water and juice. Make it clear in the joining instructions what people must bring themselves, particularly if there is no canteen on site. It is usually impractical to ask people to go to a canteen for a coffee break as travel time means that the break tends to extend, or to be so brief as to be of little value.

As with all aspects of the RPIW, keep to time. Start at the agreed time after a break. If someone joins late acknowledge their arrival but do not restart the session. A facilitator can offer to catch them up on what they missed at the first opportunity. Taking five minutes to precis the part that was missed, in the presence of all participants, uses up an hour of staff time if there are 12 participants (12 × 5 minutes). This would be disrespectful of staff time.

Occasionally a staff member, usually senior, will see dropping in and out of sessions as their right, and will expect things to be stopped, repeated and even re-run for them. This is not acceptable and is disrespectful of other participants. The facilitators can remind them of the ground rules. If they cannot agree, or agree but continue to behave in this way, then they may have to leave the RPIW. If they feel they just do not have the time, for example because they have been left with other duties, the

facilitators can escalate this to the Sponsor who can decide whether to remove the other duties, or to remove the person from the RPIW. This is distinct from pre-agreed absences or from family emergencies that require a person to leave the RPIW which do happen from time to time and cannot be avoided.

Training in Lean Techniques

In most organisations staff will need to be introduced to Lean techniques. The rest of Day One is devoted to teaching. Table 8.2 expands on the outline in Table 8.1 and describes the kind of teaching content that can be useful to include.

Some organisations may teach some of these matters in other settings, particularly techniques such as error-proofing and the use of root cause analysis and Plan-Do-Study-Act (PDSA) cycles. If so, these can be summarised or omitted altogether. It is often worth reminding people of the principles, but there is no need to dwell on issues people already understand. There are other issues that can be relevant to individual RPIWs and information on these topics can be added in as required.

Our previous book, by the same publisher, *Applying Lean in Health and Social Care Services* can be used as a sourcebook to use to design teaching materials (Stark & Hookway, 2019). Books in the reading list at the end of this volume are other useful sources for teaching ideas.

PowerPoint presentations have their place, and some knowledge is necessary to allow people to participate in the RPIW to the best of their ability. Teaching also helps to even out knowledge imbalances within the team if some staff have previous exposure to Lean techniques. Making the sessions interesting and keeping people engaged is essential. Techniques to help with this include:

■ Use plenty of examples. If the facilitators do not yet have examples from their own organisation to discuss, use examples from the literature, from books and from case reports. Stark and Hookway (2019) and Mead et al. (2023) have numerous examples that can be used.

■ Link topics to the RPIW subject. Where there are topics that relate directly to the RPIW, make the point if the group does not recognise the link spontaneously. Do this carefully so that it does not feel as if the facilitators are dictating the direction in which the RPIW should travel, but rather are noting themes that have emerged during the preparatory work.

■ Incorporate practical exercises. These are not necessary for every topic but are good to use when

Table 8.2 Possible Teaching Sequence

Topic	Content Summary
Introduction to Lean	Summary of the main principles, and demonstration of how the principles integrate.
Value and Waste	Cover this topic early in the presentation, as the approach builds naturally on the concept. Use this as a chance to populate the waste wheel. Ask the group to fill in as many sticky notes as they can, with one waste per note, and to add them to the waste wheel. The facilitators can read out the wastes that have been identified and note any common themes. Where necessary ideas can be moved between categories of waste, explaining why this is done.
5S	This is a practical topic and easy to demonstrate. Almost all RPIWs include some aspect of 5S and allowing people to start to think about it early is useful. Make sure that the description explains that the same thinking can be applied to subjects like electronic filing and that the idea is not confined to physical objects. Undertaking a 5S exercise works well in getting people moving about and undertaking some teamwork. There are commercial exercises available, and suggestions for exercises that can be homemade can be found online.
Visual Controls	People find visual controls intuitive and enjoy hearing about them and seeing examples. Showing a wider range of examples can help people to identify opportunities that the team may not have considered.
Error-Proofing	Discuss the role of error-proofing and common approaches to reducing errors. This is a good time to emphasise the focus on systems rather than individuals.
Set-Up Reduction	Set-up reduction is a common theme in RPIWs. Preparing theatres, clinic rooms, laboratories, kitchens, etc., all benefit from set-up reduction, and set up and tear-down delays are often identified as problems. There are several set-up reduction exercises available and keeping exercises leavened into the day helps to avoid drifts in attention and to keep people engaged.
PDSA Cycles	PDSA Cycles are core to any quality improvement approach and will be used during the RPIW. Distribute copies of any forms that the organisation uses for PDSA cycles. Emphasise the measurement elements of a PDSA cycle.
Standard Work	Explain the components and value of Standard Work. Include a discussion of concerns about reduced clinical freedom. Allow people the opportunity to discuss any concerns.
Flow	This gives an opportunity to explain flow, to discuss takt time and to illustrate cycle times and lead times. Incorporating an exercise on basic recording and timing of work cycles is helpful and allows people to practice with stopwatches or phone/tablet Apps and Direct Observation Records.
Levelling	Levelling sometimes comes as a revelation to people. The explicit consideration of capacity and demand, and a discussion of levelling demand and making changes to systems when demand cannot be levelled are relevant to many situations in an RPIW.
Value Stream Maps	Link the ideas together by describing the components of a Value Stream Map. This will also be useful for ownership of the outcome of the RPIW, which will include a revised VSM.
A3 Forms	Some organisations introduce A3 forms as part of the training. The Project Form used in many RPIWs is very similar and can be used to introduce the idea.
Management	Introducing Lean Management and describing how it operates at scale can help people to see how parts of a system link together. It is also a good time to discuss the maintenance of gains over time and how management methods can support both maintenance of change and the identification and testing of further improvements to the service.

possible. Try to make exercises team endeavours where members of the team are put into groups for the exercise. This lets people meet others, allows people to ask one another questions and begins to model the group work that will be key to the success of the RPIW.

■ Make it easy for the participants to ask questions and to raise points they find unclear or are doubtful about. Lean is not about Groupthink. Dissent and discussion are valuable and may produce insights for the whole team. Take time to explain a point when it is unclear. Rephrasing and adding illustrations are often helpful.

■ Encourage team members to capture ideas that arise during the presentations. Make sure there is a plentiful supply of Ideas Forms. Some teams produce 60 or more ideas for improvement during teaching. They do not need to discuss them or even to share them in detail at this stage, but make it clear that they are welcome. Encourage people to capture the idea and collect them for use in the remainder of the RPIW. Pause at the end of each section and remind people to record any ideas that have been prompted by that session's content.

■ Get the pacing right. There is a lot to get through and the day can be tiring. Give people scheduled breaks. Make sure the sessions restart on time. This sets an important precedent for the rest of the week.

Linking Back to the Workshop Aims

The day began with a statement of the issues and a review of the data. Throughout the day, the facilitators will seek to link the teaching to the problems. Towards the end of the afternoon, it is important to give the participants an opportunity to look again at their current state, in the light of the teaching.

Creating a diagram of the current process is a good way to do this. The method to develop a process diagram is described in Chapter 5 and is sometimes done as an earlier pre-workshop session if time permits. If it has been done already, the Process Owner or one of the facilitators can run through the diagram. If not, the diagram can be created in the Day One workshop using the method described. If it is to be done on the day, additional time will have to be incorporated and other sections reduced or removed to make it fit.

Have a ready supply of Ideas Forms and remind people to fill one in any time they have an idea. The combination of the Data Walk, the teaching and the development or review of the diagram often prompt many new ideas.

> **BOX 8.3 PRACTICE TIP –
> CURRENT STATE DIAGRAM**
>
> When creating the Current State diagram, participants often want to begin to change it. The facilitators should welcome this but note that the purpose is to have a record of the current process before any changes are made. Encourage people with ideas to fill in an Ideas Form.

Preparing the Team for Day Two

At the end of Day One, take time to remind the group of what has been covered. Note the wastes the team has identified, and the ideas they have generated. Reflect on the challenge from the Sponsor. Run over the structure of the rest of the week, and signpost the work for the next day, which will include designing a new process and beginning to test out the changes. Suggest that people note any ideas they have overnight and bring them back tomorrow. Remind people about timekeeping.

Ask them to write on sticky notes what has gone well today, and what could be improved. Ask the team members to add them to wall chart. Read out the notes and summarise any themes. If there are things that can be responded to at once, do so. The facilitators should not be defensive. If, for example, some participants note frustration about speed of change, with much of the day spent in teaching, acknowledge this and link it to the work for the following day.

Ask participants to tick a smiley face/neutral face/sad face wall chart to illustrate their feelings about the day as they leave the room.

Debrief and Preparation for Day Two

The facilitators should debrief on the day once the participants have left. They should consider what went well and what could be improved. Identify any emergent themes, either on team functioning or on the topic of the RPIW. The Process Owner may wish to be involved in the debriefing, and this will become progressively more important as the week progresses.

Review the feedback on the sticky notes and on the smiley face chart. There may be issues that can be resolved overnight, such as a room being too hot or too cold, lack of availability of water or similar practical issues. Making immediate changes in response to feedback can demonstrate a willingness to make changes to reflect staff experience. Staff are often surprised when a problem in the room has been resolved overnight. Other things raised can be discussed later in the week if required or fed back to the planning of future RPIWs if they raise points about organisation or teaching content.

If some people have been very quiet, the facilitators can agree that one of them will make a point of speaking to those people individually the following day to establish if they have any specific concerns, or if there are any elements of the RPIW that are making them uncomfortable.

Get the room back into its layout for the following day and agree on what time the facilitators will reconvene in the morning. This will usually be later than on Day One as there will be less to arrange, and the team members will know where they are going. Being in the room and ready at least 30 minutes before the start time is helpful as it gives the opportunity to chat with any early arrivals. This allows the facilitators to take the temperature of the event, gives participants an opportunity to make comments in a smaller group and helps the facilitators and team members to get to know one another.

References

Mead, E., Stark, C., Thompson, M. (2023). *International examples of lean in healthcare: Case studies of best practices.* Routledge.

Stark, C., & Hookway, G. (2019). *Applying lean in health and social care services.* Routledge.

Recommended Sources for Lean Teaching

Barnas, K., & Adams, E. (2014). *Beyond heroes: A lean management system for healthcare.* Thedacare Centre for Healthcare Value.

Bicheno, J. (2008). *The lean toolbox for service systems.* PICSIE Books.

Black, J. R., Miller, D. (2008). *The Toyota way to healthcare excellence.* Health Administration Press.

Graban, M. (2016). *Lean hospitals* (3rd ed.). Routledge.

Graban, M. (2019). *Measures of success.* Constancy Inc.

Graban, M., & Swartz, J. E. (2012). *Healthcare Kaizen: Engaging front-line staff in sustainable continuous improvements.* CRC Press.

Jackson, T. L. (Ed.). (2009). *5S for healthcare.* Productivity Press.

Jackson, T. L. (Ed.). (2012). *Standard work for lean healthcare.* Productivity Press.

Jackson, T. L. (Ed.). (2013a). *Kaizen workshops for lean healthcare.* Productivity Press.

Jackson, T. L. (Ed.). (2013b). *Mapping clinical value streams.* Productivity Press.

Kenney, C. (2011). *Transforming health care: Virginia Mason medical centre's pursuit of the perfect patient experience.* Productivity Press.

Kenney, C. (2015). *A leadership journey in health care: Virginia Mason's story.* CRC Press.

Martin, K., & Osterling, M. (2014). *Value stream mapping: How to visualize work and align leadership for organizational transformation.* McGraw-Hill.

Mead, E., Stark, C., & Thompson, M. (2023). *International examples of lean in healthcare: Case studies of best practices.* Routledge.

Ohno, T. (1988). *Toyota production system: Beyond large-scale production.* CRC Press.

Orelio, A. (2020). *Lean thinking for emerging healthcare leaders.* Business Expert Press.

Pyzdek, T. (2021). *The lean healthcare handbook: A complete guide to creating healthcare workplaces.* Springer Nature.

Productivity Press Development Team. (1996). *5S for operators: 5 pillars of the visual workplace.* Productivity Press.

Rother, M. (2010). *Toyota Kata: Managing people for improvement, adaptiveness, and superior results.* McGraw-Hill.

Rother, M., & Shook, J. (1999). *Learning to see.* Lean Enterprise Institute.

Sobek, D. K., & Smalley, A. (2008). *Understanding A3 thinking: A critical component of Toyota's PDCA management system.* Productivity Press.

Stark, C., & Hookway, G. (2019). *Applying lean in health and social care services.* Routledge.

Toussaint, J. S., & Adams, E. (2015). *Management on the mend.* ThedaCare Center for Healthcare Value.

Womack, J. P., & Jones, D. T. (2003). *Lean thinking: Banish waste and create wealth in your corporation.* Simon & Schuster.

Zidel, T. G. (2006) *Lean guide to transforming healthcare: How to implement lean principles in hospitals, medical offices, clinics, and other healthcare organizations.* ASQ Quality Press.

Chapter 9

Day Two

Introduction

Day Two is at least as important as Day One. It sets the tone for the actions in the rest of the week and acts as a link between the teaching and background information from the preparatory work and Day One, and the action-oriented work of Day Three and Day Four.

Sitting in a classroom is a familiar situation to most health and social care staff and can bring assumptions about what is expected. It is easy to debate options with no immediate pressure to do anything and people often find this comfortable. Moving to a commitment to change and to actively test out options is a more challenging and stressful situation. Teams often need support to move from discussion to action, and Day Two should be structured to help this happen.

The aim of the facilitators on Day Two is to shake off any passivity that might have arisen during the teaching day. RPIWs are about change, and it is important to help people to apply the training and the collected information to their own situation, to reach an agreement about a way ahead and to start work on practical improvements.

An outline of a Day-Two agenda is shown in Table 9.1. It should be taken as indicative. Facilitators will create their own agenda and timings to meet the needs of the team and the event.

Preparation

The two facilitators and ideally the Process Owner should meet well before the scheduled start time. Time flies by when getting things ready, and participants may begin to arrive as well, so arriving an hour early is likely to give time to check things over and discuss any ideas which have arisen overnight.

Check over the room to confirm that everything is in place. Janitorial staff may move items as part of their routine, and the room arrangement may need to be changed back to the layout required for the purposes of the workshop. It is also worth checking on any areas that have been identified as break-out spaces, to ensure that they are still available. If an area can no longer be used, it will be necessary to find a replacement. Sometimes people on the RPIW will work in a nearby office that is empty for the duration of the event, and this can be appropriated at short notice. Sympathetic local managers can also help to identify replacement spaces.

Think about the flow of the meeting. Items on the wall may need to be moved if this was not done the previous evening. The data wall and Current State Map should be visible, and a space is needed to put the developing Ideal Future State diagram. This needs to be in a place which is visible and where people can gather around it. Some facilitators prefer to leave the blank Future State diagram down until it is needed but take the time to work out where it will go and what you will move.

If not done the previous evening, put a rough agenda for the day on a flip chart. Knowing when lunch and breaks will be and the expected time to finish is useful for participants in setting their expectations for the structure of the day.

Greet participants as they arrive. People understand that facilitators need to work to ready an event, but it is courteous to welcome participants back, and to check that no new questions arose overnight. If a participant thought of a new idea overnight, encourage them to complete an Ideas Form.

DOI: 10.4324/9780429020742-9

Table 9.1   Example of a Day-Two Agenda

0900	Daily debrief
0915	Review of the Current State Design the Future State
10.20	Break
10.35	Agree on Work Streams Check Ideas and Wastes Allocate Groups Workgroups begin work
12.10	Report Back from Workgroups
12.30	Lunchbreak
13.10	Workgroups Facilitators visit groups – further Report Back if required
14.50	Break
15.00	Workgroups Facilitators visit groups
15.55	Report Back from Workgroups
16.15	Team Members leave for the day
16.20	Sponsor meeting with Process Owner and Facilitators
16.45	Day Ends

Opening Session

Welcome people back. Take a few minutes to ask them their reflections on Day One, and for any ideas or thoughts that occurred to them overnight.

Review the comments on the previous day and acknowledge any concerns or suggestions. If any practical changes, for example to housekeeping arrangements, have been made because of the suggestions, then report them back so that the group knows that action has been taken.

If one or more people have indicated on the exit survey that they were unhappy with Day One, it is worth asking if anyone wants to share their disappointments or concerns if this has not already come up. This is not an attempt to identify people for any punitive reason, but rather to acknowledge that one or more people were not happy and to seek to learn from it.

There are common concerns that are reported. As discussed in the previous chapter, these include guilt that other people are working in the service while they have 'a week off'. This is straightforward to respond to: the week

---

BOX 9.1   PRACTICE TIP – LISTENING TO THE ROOM

The facilitators need to have one eye on the clock throughout the day and to pay careful attention to thieves of time: circular debate, procrastination and active or passive obstruction of change. The corollary is that the facilitators must not ride roughshod over the group in their own urgency to move things on. People fearing change is common, but sometimes there is a reason why things feel sticky.

If there is great difficulty in moving on, it is essential to take stock of what is happening. It may be that there is something that has not been identified in the preparation, often relating to team dynamics. Teasing out the nature of any concerns and making them explicit is necessary. In the light of day, concerns often fade or prove to be not so worrying. From time to time, real issues come up that need to be considered such as rarely discussed concerns within a team about some historical incident, such as '*the time we ran out of item x because there was a strike / it snowed / the van broke down*', or occasionally about the performance or personality of an individual. The Process Owner will usually have identified any such issues in advance, but this is not always the case.

If there are undercurrents about an individual, the facilitators may have to ask the Process Owner to work with the issue as best they can. It is not appropriate to prompt discussion in the wider session about an individual – the focus should be on the process – but the Process Owner or relevant line manager may need to meet with a person to seek to resolve any concerns. If a larger issue emerges, such as previously unknown concerns around the behaviour of a person, then this will need to be followed up using the appropriate organisational procedures, after the workshop.

There are other, more predictable, issues such as worries over changes to the role of a staff group or an individual. These need to be dealt with sensitively. Usually, personal conversations can resolve concerns, particularly when a change to processes is in the interests of service users.

Power relationships can be important and simmering issues in a team can get in the way if they are not acknowledged and dealt with. Sometimes it is best to acknowledge an issue and to accept that it is outside the scope of the RPIW but needs attention. It is usually possible to obtain a commitment from the relevant senior staff to address non-RPIW-related concerns in a timely manner.

will be hard work, and they have been identified as participants because the Process Owner and the facilitators believe they have a lot to offer. This concern sometimes masks worry that the people working in the service will be annoyed at them, or that the participant will be blamed for any problems that arise from changes. If this seems to be relevant, it is useful to note that the people working in the service will take part in the testing of any changes and will have the opportunity to introduce further changes and refinements after the RPIW.

Another concern can be inaction. Day One can feel like a classroom session and some participants may be frustrated at the perceived lack of progress on Day One. This worry can be acknowledged and used to emphasise the need for progress and focus during the remainder of the RPIW.

Other concerns that are offered can be acknowledged even if there is no direct action that can be taken or if it is an isolated concern for one person. Listening to the concerns and being seen to take them seriously is helpful in modelling the behaviours that will allow the RPIW to succeed, which will help the team to make changes over longer periods. Shouting down or ignoring concerns is never helpful.

Another less often stated but often present concern are worries about getting things done. When people have time to take stock of the challenges in a service, it can feel overwhelming. The changes required can feel impossibly large and this can lead to an unwillingness to get started because the weight of change and the pressure of expectations on the event seems crushing. The RPIW structure is designed to help teams to prioritise actions and to break activities down into manageable pieces. Reminding people that this is a group endeavour, that the whole burden does not rest on an individual, and that the RPIW is not expected to resolve every difficulty helps to provide some reassurance.

The future state the team developed at this session is the framework for the remainder of the week. The group is not tied to it: if they produce a new idea, it can be incorporated, but often there will be no major changes during the remainder of the week, emphasising the importance of this session.

Run Back over the Current State

Take a few minutes to run back through the Current State Process Diagram. If this was not completed the previous day, finish it as quickly as practical. Running back over the diagram reminds participants of what they agreed and acts as a springboard into the development of the Ideal Future State.

Ideal Future State Process Map

The purpose of this session is to give the team time to envisage an Ideal Future State which would resolve the problems identified in the run-up to the RPIW and which were shared on Day One. This Ideal Future State then provides an aspiration for the basis of the remainder of the RPIW: what can the group do to move as close to this future state as possible?

Use the same method as was used for the development of the Current State Map. Please see Chapter 5 for details. When people have worked in the same system for some time, and often for many years, it can be difficult for them to envisage something markedly different. Early discussion often features ideas for marginal change. If small changes were all that were needed, incremental quality improvement would usually have uncovered them already. The facilitators need to help the team to think beyond minor changes to a more radical redesign.

Imposing some arbitrary constraints can be helpful. People often want to do more of what they do already. People often feel that if five staff working on a function is good, then ten staff will be twice as good. This is tempting and, on some occasions, will be right. The problem for an RPIW is that this approach and the assumption of existing correctness constrain creativity. Scaling up the current system which is already causing problems is a common organisational response to capacity limitations. If the system is perfect, or there is a major constraint that can be eased, then this may work. More often there are already wastes in the system that are not addressed by simply adding more resources. Often additional resource complicates the existing problems by adding further complexity or by layering processes one on the other without first resolving any existing issues.

This does not mean that additional resource is never required. Developing a good process and reducing wastes combined with a vision of what is required make a far stronger case for additional resources if it remains impossible to deliver what is needed.

In the design phase of the RPIW, a mantra of *'no new staff, no new equipment, no new money'* repeated as often as necessary works well. This requires staff to work on their processes to achieve the required gains. One of the authors facilitated an RPIW in which the group argued for addressing queues in the process by doubling the size of the waiting room by extending into an outdoor courtyard. The Lean reasons – and the human reasons – why this is inappropriate are apparent. Imposing constraints on resources helps to avoid this kind of solution.

The method of producing process diagrams is discussed in Chapter 5. As noted, try not to let people settle down into an abstract exercise where no conclusions are reached. Putting the paper on a wall and asking people to come over to the wall help to keep people standing and engaging, accepting that arrangements will be needed for anyone who is physically unable to stand for an hour or more.

When people present their ideas, test them out against the wastes identified. Consider whether the ideas address the wastes. As noted, teams often begin by offering incremental changes to existing processes. Encourage the team to think of the ideal process from the perspective of the person using the service. Service user participants can explain the difficulties caused by delays and complications.

There is an art to describing an Ideal Future State, and the facilitators can help by reminding people of the teaching from Day One and referring to any wastes identified. For example, if staff want to add a step to check referrals, the facilitators can inquire whether the step adds value and encourage the group to consider what steps could be put in place to reduce errors in referrals before they arrive. If there are duplication or waits in the new process, ask how these can be reduced.

A tension for participants is imagining a future state but worrying that is it unobtainable. They may also be concerned that if they create a design, they cannot reach then they will be criticised for not getting there. A response to this is to emphasise the role of the organisation in supporting change and the role of the Sponsor in working with the group over time to achieve change. A reminder about the Friday Report Out and the senior engagement they can expect can help. The facilitators can explain the collective responsibility for delivery, with the Process Owner escalating blockages to the Sponsor over the coming months. If the staff group deals with the issues within their own control, then they should be assured that they will not be blamed for blocks to progress from outside their area of control.

Work through the whole new process with the staff. Discourage endless 'what if' discussions where every possible objection and remote possibility event is considered. Taking a Pareto approach, with a focus on the main pathways that happen for most patients, most of the time, can help to keep people on track. Asking how often a situation arises and then reminding staff of the benefits of improving the big volume pathways first works. Noting that improving the flow and reducing waste in high-volume activities will, in turn, free up time that can be applied to more complex situations and can offer some reassurance.

Where there are unresolved concerns, or a person finds it very difficult to move on from an objection, remind the group that they will have the opportunity to test changes out and if a change does not work in practice, it can be changed. Identifying balancing measures that will allow the group to keep track of a possible risk can also be useful, although this may be better done over the following days as a reassurance.

Try hard not to let the future state map development become an academic exercise with little link to change. It is easy and sometimes comfortable to discuss things in the abstract and to consider objections in minute detail. Some people like to feel they have won an argument with

a *bon mot*: remind people of the agreed ground rules. The purpose of the event is to create change to benefit service users, not to win a debate. The only real test of a plausible idea is to try it out and the facilitators need to move people on to action.

Watch out for people who seem distant from the process, or who engage only to throw in the occasional objection. The spirit of an RPIW is to discuss issues in the open and to share concerns, but with an overall intention of achieving improvement. People who say little may be intimidated by more senior staff or may have previous experience of their views being disregarded. Consider asking them their views on points particularly relevant to their current role. It goes without saying that the facilitators should listen with respect to their response. Making a point of taking every intervention seriously no matter the organisational role of the contributor helps to make the egalitarian ethos of an RPIW clear to everyone. Lean principles assume that the people who are closest to the process understand the most about it. Model the behaviour you want to see.

Silence can also indicate passive opposition. This needs to be checked out. RPIWs are not a place for silence. If the person sees a problem that has eluded others, they can help by sharing it and so preventing unnecessary effort. From time to time, the issue proves to be anxiety. This can relate to change itself or to the specifics of a particular change. For example, if a step is identified as waste and removed, this may represent a person's job. They may be understandably worrying about the impact on themselves. This may need to be dealt within the group, or one to one. For RPIWs to be effective, staff need to be secure in the knowledge that they will not lose their job because of the improvement activity. This does not mean that a role may not change, or a person may need to be redeployed elsewhere. Even a modest change to their work activities may feel threatening and distressing.

The facilitators need to keep an eye out for unstated concerns and address them as best they can. The worries of one person, if they do not relate to a problem in the new process, cannot be allowed to derail improvements, but Lean is underpinned by respect for staff and understanding and addressing as far as possible staff concerns is an important part of the work of an RPIW.

Moving to Action

Once the group has a likely future state map, congratulate the group on their effort. This is usually a good time to take a break. It is sometimes necessary to re-jig the timetable on Day Two depending on how long essential steps take but keeping a feeling of momentum is essential. Aiming to complete the future state by mid-morning is helpful.

BOX 9.2 PRACTICE TIP – WORKING WITH ANXIETY

As noted above, anxiety may be linked to the RPIW process and can be dealt with by clarity and reassurance. Mental health problems are common, however, so people with anxiety disorders will sometimes find themselves in an RPIW.

Challenges for a workshop participant may become apparent during the development phase of the RPIW, but in some cases, it is not visible to the coaches until the event itself. If someone seems to be experiencing challenges with the social situation and the decision-making process, it is important not to leave them to suffer unaided. The facilitators have a duty of care towards the participants.

It is usually possible to support the person to have a successful experience from the RPIW. Chat to the person to establish the nature of the problem away from other participants and then work out how to support them. Often reassurance that they can take part in a way that works for them is sufficient. Not everyone has to report back on actions in the previous session, but this does not mean that they must be excluded from the improvement work or that they lose the opportunity to contribute ideas.

The Friday Report Out is sometimes a worry as some people dread any public speaking. Reassurance that their input can be very brief can help, although sometimes by the time the Friday Report Out comes along, people feel more able to speak having been involved throughout the week. The facilitators should keep an eye out for any ongoing problems and check in with the person regularly to ensure that they are coping and are not unduly distressed.

If this does not seem to have been a problem that has been identified previously, it is appropriate to discuss with the person whether support may be needed after the RPIW including signposting to Occupational Health services. The opportunity to work closely with someone and so identify the challenges they are experiencing may bring benefits by allowing the person to talk about their problem and to be referred on for definitive treatment.

Thinking Time for the Facilitators and Process Owners

Use the break for the facilitators and the Process Owner to think about the likely work streams, and to think about what staff are needed for which workstream. This is not an attempt to exclude people from contributing to an idea that attracts them, but rather to match a range of people to pieces of work that they can influence. Some staff might want to be involved in all workstreams, but this is not possible. There is too much to do in an RPIW for this to be practical. Everyone will have the opportunity to make suggestions and to hear about progress in each workstream, but activities must be done in parallel rather than as a series of episodes of work which can involve everyone in each stage.

First, identify the likely work components. The work on an Ideal Future State will have illustrated areas in which work is required. For example, there may be work on a referral process, on scheduling of investigations, on reporting of results and on delays within a clinic process. This is likely to further break down into more manageable tasks. In the outpatient services example, the referral process improvements may include new guidelines for referrers; a system to stream referrals by urgency or by subtype; changes to the booking process, changes to information provided to people attending the clinic, and so on. The subsequent discussion with the team may change the work packets, but it is very helpful for the facilitators to have a rough list of required areas of work at their fingertips as they can use it as a checklist to avoid things being missed.

Having a rough feel for how work might be divided up within the team is useful. When identifying possible staff, think about the groups of functions that are involved in each process. For example, improvement work on referral processes and referral handling is likely to involve both administrative staff and clinicians. Work on arranging supplies in outpatient rooms may need several grades of nurses, other relevant clinicians and possibly support staff, and so on. Avoid having people who do not work in that part of the process taking decisions on behalf of those who undertake the process every day. Others may have a valuable input and may be assisted by gaining a better understanding of the process, but the people who do the job are essential to the review of the work.

Having people who work in a neighbouring process involved in a group can be helpful as they may be able to contribute information about what happens before or after the stage being reviewed. This helps to know what information and activities are important and can also give the person working in the neighbouring process ideas about how they could improve flow, reduce defects and avoid waste in their own service.

Often numbers do not quite work out for the work group allocation, and there is more than one piece of work that would benefit from the participation of people with the same skills. Make pragmatic decisions about this and be prepared to move people around to join other groups or to provide advice. Staff may feel that they can contribute more to a different workgroup, but they may need to assist with a particular issue first. People understand this when it is discussed openly and respectfully.

Review Ideas Forms and Agree Workstreams

Once the group are back together, review the Ideas Forms in the light of the Ideal Future State the team have developed. Try to have the team participate as much as possible. Avoid the impression that the facilitators are there to make decisions for the service. Distributing forms so that each person reads out a few can work well. Agree with the team on what themes are included and group them into appropriate categories. Some people actively enjoy this and may spontaneously begin to collect grouped forms. This is fine as long as one or two people do not take over the whole process.

Some of the groupings will be method categories, for example, comments about Flow, 5S or Standard Work. In other cases, it may make more sense to group ideas into stages of a process – for example, referral, triage, appointment scheduling, etc. The group may revise categories as they read more forms. This is beginning to lay out workstreams that the team agree on. The facilitators should use their pre-work over the previous break to allow them to identify if anything striking is missing from the list compared to the changes identified in the future state session.

At all stages check that the ideas get the team closer to the Ideal Future State. There may be good ideas which do not relate to the main areas of focus of the RPIW. These can be kept in a 'parking lot' and passed to the Process Owner at the end of the RPIW to schedule work on them. Some good ideas may have been overtaken by events. For example, some ideas may relate to a stage of the process which the team has already agreed to remove, or to a problem with a process that is being tackled with a different change.

Review Wastes and Match Them to Ideas

Once the ideas are considered, look again at the Waste Wheel. Consider which ideas address which wastes. Match the wastes to the ideas, so that sub-groups can take both the wastes and ideas away. This also gives a good impression of any wastes which are not addressed by any improvement ideas, and which may need to be picked up later in the RPIW or during the follow-up phase.

Look back at the Future State Value Stream Map. Consider whether the plan covers most or all the wastes and the ideas. This is an opportunity to make amendments to the map if required. Sometimes an idea is so persuasive that the team wants to make an amendment to the future state map.

Launch Workstreams

Explain that there will be a series of workstreams, and that people will move between groups both as tasks are completed, and if their skills are needed in other groups. Make it clear that people will not stay in the same group for the rest of the week so that a move does not come as a surprise when it happens.

It is helpful to begin to group workstreams and the smaller tasks within each workstream. For example, a workstream on flow may involve several stages and perhaps pieces of work on error reduction. Using large adhesive notes on a whiteboard or flip chart gives a visual impression of how the pieces of work fit together, what has been done and what remains to be tackled (Figure 9.1).

Prioritise the workstreams and activities. This depends both on importance and on interconnections. There may be some major gains to be made relatively easily and it makes sense to prioritise these. In other cases, some steps

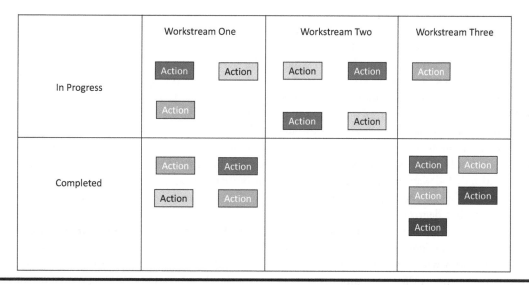

Figure 9.1   Tracking workstreams

must be made before another action can happen, which means that they must be sequenced. In many other instances work on different parts of the workstream can take place at the same time with no interaction. If there is disagreement about priority, then a prioritisation matrix can be used as a group process to seek agreement (Box 9.3).

Describe the workstream groups that the facilitators and Process Owner identified during the break and check that people are willing to work on these areas. There is room for negotiation, but sometimes it will be necessary to ask a person with relevant knowledge to take part in a group that is not their preference. Be open about this, explain why and agree with the person on how they can link into their other topic of interest.

Once the groups are identified, agree on where they will work. People may work in different sections of a large room but sometimes they will work in other areas and very soon the groups will be breaking off to try out changes in practice. Getting into the habit of identifying where people are going is invaluable so that time is not wasted locating people or groups. Having a flip chart where each group notes its new location helps with this. Agree on a time to return to report on progress and stick to it. See the Practice Tips on timekeeping.

Before groups leave to begin work on the ideas and actions check that they have what they need. This can include paper, adhesive notes, information collected in the preparation phase, PDSA forms and so on. It is easier if they take this with them rather than come back to locate it. The facilitators are likely to have an idea of what might be needed and can help the groups to take with them what they need.

Workgroups

When the workgroups begin, there is no respite for the facilitators. They need to check on the workgroups to keep track of progress, to act as runners to connect the groups, to answer questions and to help on Lean techniques and thinking.

The facilitators can agree on who will check on which group, and they may stick to this or exchange groups depending on progress and other demands on their time. The Process Owner will usually be part of a workgroup as they may not have the background to allow them to offer technical Lean advice to groups.

The facilitators should agree when they will meet to discuss progress, usually halfway through the time agreed for the groups to work before coming back together. The groups will need varying degrees of input. This will be affected by how much previous experience the groups have of Lean and of RPIWs. Experienced groups may need very little input. Other groups will need more. This will also vary over the course of the RPIW: more input is usually needed on Day Two than on Day Four for example.

BOX 9.3   PRIORITISATION MATRIX

A prioritisation matrix can be used to promote group agreement and to make visible any disagreements.

Agree with the group on two dimensions to be used to prioritise improvement actions. Common dimensions would be impact and difficulty – how big an impact on the problem would the action have if it was completed, and how difficult is it likely to be to complete it? These dimensions are not set in stone, and it may be appropriate to vary them to suit the situation.

Draw a cross on a flipchart as shown in Figure 9.2. If using standard dimensions, label one axis as 'Impact' and the other as 'difficulty'. This gives a two-by-two grid. The top right box is for actions which would have high impact and are thought to be relatively easy to complete, the bottom left box is for low-impact, high-difficulty actions and so on.

Take each potential action in turn, write it on a sticky note, and ask the group to agree on where it should be placed. Within squares, there can be differences in impact and ease, moving actions within the square.

Generally, the group will agree not to advance actions that they see as low impact and high difficulty. Actions that are high impact and relatively easy are very likely to be agreed. There will be trade-offs for items in other boxes, so a more difficult action that is of high impact may be prioritised, or a group may decide to pick up an action that is of lower impact but is very straightforward to undertake.

This helps to tease out group agreement on options, and to make it clear to everyone why a particular action has been prioritised over other options.

When facilitators drop into a group, it is best to let the participants proceed rather than interjecting straight away. The group may be doing well and will often think of things that have not occurred to the facilitators. It is important that the facilitators do not take over the groups when they visit them. Part of the legacy of an RPIW should be the knowledge that the team developed, tested and implemented changes. This can be lost if the facilitators are overly assertive with their own ideas.

Issues to consider with groups include:

■ **The opportunity to participate.** Is everyone involved? Are any group members being excluded, deliberately or accidentally? If so, the facilitators can bring them back into the discussion, for example by asking their opinion on a point, or referring to their

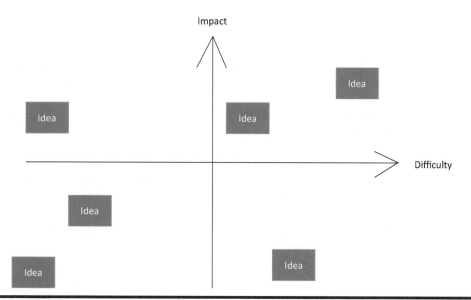

Figure 9.2   Example of a Prioritisation Matrix

expertise. Ensure that any patient/carer/advocacy group representatives are involved in discussions and in tests of change.

■ **Moving to action.** The opportunity to discuss and debate is important, but it is essential to move to action. The balance between discussion and action is difficult to prescribe, but too much time spent in debate can be a sign that the group is uneasy about testing changes out. This can be down to embarrassment, uncertainty or inertia. Encouragement to work out how to test a change is often all that is required to get things moving. Going with a work group to the workplace to get started may be required.

■ **Using PDSA cycles**. Debate is all very well, but the test of an idea is whether it works in practice. Clarity on the outcome is essential, and teams must be encouraged to use PDSA cycles. The use of a PDSA cycle, and associated forms, helps to define the intervention; who will undertake it; what is expected to happen and how the change will be measured. An explicit comparison of the expected impact to what happened in practice is necessary. If the expected change does not happen as anticipated, this is information that can be fed into the next attempt at change. Teams learn more from a PDSA cycle, whether it achieves the expected outcome or not, than from further debate. An example of a form to record PDSA cycles is shown in Figure 2.5.

■ **Task drift.** Teams with a specific remit sometimes begin to second guess their task and want to look at something that is in the remit of another team. If a team has a good idea, this should be recorded, and can be fed into future task allocation. The team

needs to carry through their initial task, however, unless they quickly identify a major flaw that requires a rethink on that portion of the process. Even then, the team can be encouraged to work out and test an alternative way of achieving the desired effect.

■ **Reference to relevant techniques.** The facilitators can direct the group towards methods discussed on Day One that are relevant to their current work. This is a good opportunity to let participants see how a method can be used in practice. Standard Work forms, Skills Matrices and Direct Observation Records are commonly used, in addition to PDSA forms. It saves time if the facilitators carry a folder with a set of commonly used forms that they can distribute as required. Reminding people of principles, such as error proofing, can also be required and the facilitators may need to support groups to work through calculations, such as takt time.

Testing Out Changes in Practice

It is common for health and social care services to make changes, but to have no clear evidence that the change has the desired effect. In quality improvement work, PDSA cycles are the key to knowing if a process change has an impact. This is not the same as knowing if the overall outcome of an event is achieved, but if the underlying theory of change relies on many small process changes, then knowing that the process changes have occurred is essential.

PDSA cycles, discussed in Chapter 2, are central to the RPIW process and to quality improvement in general.

BOX 9.4   PRACTICE TIP – TIME KEEPING

A week sounds like a long time. If using the RPIW structure outlined in this book, there are around two and half days of time to test out and revise changes. The facilitators and Process Owner must always keep this time pressure in mind. The facilitators will usually have experience of other RPIWs and have a feel for the pace required. For others, it is their first RPIW and a week will feel like a lot of time – perhaps too much time. This can lead to a lack of concern about timings. The facilitators must inject a feeling of dynamism into the event and encourage strict timekeeping.

Some of this can be set on Day One. The facilitators can ensure that they start sessions on time and end them at the planned time. On breaks, if someone is not back, the event should proceed as planned. There can be a brief catch-up if required but do not run back over everything or parts of the event will be re-run. A simple *'I'm sorry you were held up. We discussed x and we are now working on y'* will suffice.

If a latecomer wants to debate things that have happened in their absence, make it clear that the group cannot go back over the ground already covered, and offer to catch up with the person in the next break. This can be a difficult lesson for senior staff who may be used to having sections of meetings re-run for their benefit. RPIWs have an egalitarian structure and senior status in the organisation does not provide the right to derail an RPIW. If a senior staff member proves difficult, it may be necessary to involve the Sponsor in a discussion outside the RPIW sessions.

There will often be three or four workgroups operating at any one time. When the group has a catch-up session, all need to report. There are two main hazards: excessive detail and a desire by people on other groups to second guess the work of another group. On detail, it is best to model the timings required. In an early session, the facilitators may take part in a group and undertake an early report. If three groups are reporting in a 30-minute session, there may, for example, be six minutes for each report, and four minutes for any clarification or factual questions to each group. The precise timings are not important: the issue is pace, clarity and acceptance of the work of others.

One useful practice is to time the early report backs. If there are six minutes to report back, a facilitator can tell the presenter when four minutes have gone and stop them at six minutes. Tell the groups in advance that this will be done and have a word with the group that is reporting first and agree with them on what they will cover so that they do not feel exposed. Later groups will get the idea.

If a group shows a tendency to keep going with their report back, explain that it is necessary to let the other groups report, and that anyone who wants to hear more can do so in the break which often follows a report back. This can come as a surprise to people who are used to timings being said to be important, but not always being treated as such. If the facilitators persevere with it, participants adapt rapidly to the demands. It is important to keep the tone appropriate – the work is valued and having to cut a report short is not a reflection on their efforts, but rather a necessary step to maximise the impact of the week.

For questions, try hard not to let people be discouraging about the work of others. Be positive and respectful but be firm when required. Keep questions to clarifications. If someone wants to suggest an action or change for another workgroup they can do so, but they should keep it brief. There is insufficient time to have every group do all the work, which is why there are workgroups in the first place. The RPIW team must trust one another and unless someone identifies a safety issue each group should be allowed to get on with their task.

By the second half of Day Three, it is rarely necessary to remind people of timings as they will have got used to it and a gentle reminder as required will usually be sufficient to get things back on track.

Not all staff will be familiar with PDSA cycles, so support from the facilitators is important. There may be other participants with experience in the use of PDSA cycles and distributing these people between groups can be helpful in spreading and sharing expertise.

Each workgroup needs to take its currently allocated area and work out the stages it needs to go through to test out the idea. For example, if the group have been asked to develop and test a new protocol, then the stages could be:

1. Develop the protocol, consulting with topic experts as required
2. Test the text of the protocol with clinical staff
3. Test the new protocol in use to see if it has the desired effect (such as reducing potential for error, reducing omitted steps or being faster)

Each of these steps may need one or more PDSA cycles. In Step One, for example, the group may develop the protocol themselves, and then test it out with topic experts, revising as required. Testing the text for clarity and clinical response may need one test with an individual staff member and then a follow-up with two or more.

Testing the protocol in practice can start with a PDSA cycle of one staff member and one patient (assuming the protocol is for the delivery of a clinical process). This may need to be repeated, but once agreed can be tested on several patients by the same staff member. It may then need to be tested by several staff members to ensure that it is transferrable and understandable.

This type of process can easily take weeks or months in complex organisations, but in RPIWs can be conducted very quickly. The team can make instant changes based on feedback and then proceed immediately to the next PDSA cycle. Having several team members involved means that more than one clinician can be observed at once, and several people can record timings if that is an important part of the change.

The volume of work that can be undertaken can be seen when it is considered that there could be three or four groups working on changes simultaneously, for close to three working days.

BOX 9.5 PRACTICE TIP – LOGGING ACTIONS AND BEGINNING THE ACTION PLAN

The week moves very quickly in an RPIW. It is easy to forget exactly what has been trialled and what has changed. Using an action plan (sometimes called a 'newspaper' in Lean literature because it provides an update on what has happened) can help with this. The action plan will be the property of the Process Owner at the end of the event, but they may find themselves too busy to update it during the event.

One of the advantages of having two facilitators is the opportunity to spread tasks. While one facilitator is working with a group, for example, the second can take a few minutes to update the action plan.

It is useful to structure the action plan in line with the identified workstreams as it makes it easier for participants to relate to their structure of the week. Recording planned actions and the progress of them helps to keep track. If done electronically, the form can be projected during the team meet-up sessions if this seems useful. As well as showing what is to be done, it also lets participants see what they have already completed, which is easy to lose track of in the hurly-burly of an improvement event.

Involving Other Staff

Keeping the wider staff group involved and engaged is critical. If the changes are to be embraced, staff need to know that they have had opportunities to comment and to test. The Process Owner should ensure that the extended staff group are aware of the event, and the facilitators are likely to have presented the process in previous staff group meetings. A reminder on the day is valuable, and it is important not to assume that everyone is aware: a few minutes to explain what is happening when arriving in a ward or area to conduct a test will be time well spent and it also conveys respect.

There can be times when clinical activity prevents engagement, such as a ward emergency. In that case, the RPIW team should be respectful of the pressures on staff. It is generally possible to find another process or another part of the same process to work on for a few hours until it is possible to gain access. For example, if a new protocol is to be tested in practice, the draft protocol can be set aside, and the team can go back later that day when there is more opportunity for clinical staff to engage.

In the protocol example described above, when entering a ward for example a conversation with the senior nurse would be appropriate so they are sighted on what is happening in their area. They may want to select the staff to be involved, and this should be respected. Their endorsement will also be valuable in securing staff engagement.

The purpose of the proposed change should be shared with the clinical staff who are testing it out. The more they know, the more insights they will be able to share and the more involved they are likely to feel. Reassurance that the focus is not on them, but on the process can be useful, particularly when timings are involved. Encourage staff to offer qualitative feedback as well, including how the change feels in use, and how they feel it fits with other parts of the process.

There are some processes that happen too uncommonly for it to be possible to test them out in real time. In this situation, the team may need to simulate the process. This should be as realistic as possible and involve the relevant staff. When this is done, it is best to make it clear on any progress charts that simulation was used.

Sponsor Visit

The team should be encouraged to leave at the agreed time, to leave space before the Sponsor visit. When the team are in the flow of an RPIW, any seemingly adverse comment from the Sponsor can feel dispiriting. This will not be intended but having the facilitators and the Process Owner at the feedback session without the wider RPIW team usually works best.

Before the team leave, summarise the progress for the day, and agree on what people will be working on when they return the following morning. If there are any issues the team want to bring to the attention of the Sponsor, record them on a flip chart. Examples might be issues on which the team want external endorsement, or where they want help, such as the Sponsor asking for something to happen quickly in a different department or directorate, such as an IT issue. They may also want to check out their understanding of a strategic issue, and the Sponsor can help with this. As before, the team should be asked to indicate their experience of the day by ticking the appropriate box on a flip chart.

Once the team have left, it is useful for the facilitators and the Process Owner to lay things out for the visit, and to agree on what will be said. The meetings may be brief, and it is important to include everything that feels important. A possible outline would be:

- Reviewing the Project Form and the targets for the RPIW
- Reviewing the Current State
- Noting the number of wastes and ideas identified by the team
- Summarising the Future State developed by the team

- Noting the workstreams created and updating on progress
- Bringing any issues identified by the team to the attention of the Sponsor

The Sponsor will identify any issues they see on the alignment of the proposed solutions to the current and proposed actions. They may also identify additional areas related to the Future State on which they would like the team to work, including extending targets if the team have already met, or are close to meeting, the original targets. The Sponsor should also respond to all the issues raised by the team for them.

The facilitators should confirm with the Sponsor what time the Sponsor will attend on the following day.

After the Sponsor has left the facilitators and Process Owner can take stock of progress and agree on how to start the following day. They should review the entire Future State and the ongoing and planned workstreams and consider what work streams or actions to prioritise as existing actions are completed. The feedback on the flipchart should be reviewed, and any team issues considered.

They can finish by writing out a rough timetable for the following day and agreeing on when they will reconvene the following morning.

Chapter 10

Days Three and Four

Introduction

The third and fourth days of the RPIW should be the engine room in which change is tested and implemented. This section of the event also acts as a bridge to the long-term maintenance of the gains and sets the groundwork for ongoing improvement with the Process Owner. The actions of the facilitators are:

- Maintain momentum
- Support the use of Lean methods
- Record actions and improvements
- Maintain links between the workgroups
- Make use of the Advisory Group
- Update and expand targets as required
- Support a focus on the aims of the RPIW
- Keep a watchful eye on the team dynamics and provide support as required
- Work to prepare the Process Owner for the work required after the RPIW
- Maintain the housekeeping tasks
- Ensure involvement of the wider staff group
- Make use of the Sponsor

Maintaining Momentum

Keep the event and the Plan-Do-Study-Act (PDSA) cycles, moving briskly. After a successful Day Two, the team can feel they have more than enough time to complete all the tasks they have set themselves. This rarely proves to be the case. The time can pass very quickly. There are frequently actions and tests of change that cannot be conducted in the week because of time constraints. There can be a noticeable change in mood. Short, fun exercises and quick wins can be useful in bringing back the energy and enthusiasm of the Team.

The facilitators are the most likely to be aware of the time constraints because of their previous experience so it is important that they support change and encourage brisk action. This must be judged appropriately: RPIWs are a collaboration among equals rather than a schoolteacher/pupil relationship. Explanation and engagement are required. The facilitators, and the Process Owner, can also model the behaviour they want to encourage by dealing with matters within their control briskly and efficiently.

The same requirements apply as on Day One and Day Two: encourage testing rather than continued debate, and support people to move on to the next action. Having completed an action, other possible improvements are sometimes identified in the course of the work. These must be prioritised against already identified actions. Some may be smaller incremental improvements that can be undertaken by the team after the RPIW. Others may be on broader topics rather than related to the aims of the RPIW. In some instances, however, the new action will be appropriate to pursue during the RPIW. There is no hard and fast rule to apply to this. Thought, discussion and sometimes negotiation is required. Where actions are carried over for later work, they should be added to the action plan and a priority for their completion noted. If the actions are unrelated to the RPIW, they can be added to the 'Parking Lot', the list of worthwhile but unrelated improvements identified during the planning and conduct of the RPIW and passed to the Process Owner and the Sponsor for consideration, allocation and action. In some instances, they may result in further RPIWs or other smaller improvement events.

Timing of Days Three and Four

The day will be spent developing and trialling improvements. The same components as the afternoon of Day Two are required, with Report Backs to check in on progress.

DOI: 10.4324/9780429020742-10

Breaks and lunch should be scheduled, as well as start and end times. As groups will be testing out changes in the workplace, it is common for them to become desynchronised from one another as workgroups are often reluctant to stop to avoid interrupting their work. This should be accommodated but it is important to have a whole team Report Back at least once in the morning and once in the afternoon. This keeps workgroups aware of the broader work and helps to avoid duplication. It also allows people in different workgroups to comment on developments. Sharing successes across the group also helps to minimise any mid-week dip.

Support Use of Lean Methods

While quality improvement methods are common across many approaches, there are tools and approaches associated with Lean that can be applied throughout the RPIW. Carrying a supply of relevant forms as described in the previous chapters allows the facilitators to bring possible approaches to the attention of the participants when the relevant context arises.

Some common issues that arise are:

- Applying 5S, visual management and error-proofing into new processes
- Writing Standard Work in a way that is in line with the approach used in the organisation
- Keeping an eye on waste, including overprocessing
- Understanding takt time and the implications it has for process design
- Thinking through Work in Process (WIP) and Standard Work in Process (SWIP). Work in Process are the number of tests, people or whatever is relevant to the process being reviewed, who are in the system at any one time. Standard Work in Process are the number of items, or people, that need to be in the system to keep it flowing
- Linking parts of the process together to support flow, including applying buffers when required. Buffers can be important when there is a bottleneck in a process that needs to always work at maximum capacity
- Helping staff to calculate revised Lead Times

The more experience the coaches develop, the more they will feel able to support staff in applying techniques. In some RPIWs, there will be participants who have already taken part in RPIWs and undertaken previous Lean teaching, who can be involved to support other staff. Bringing someone from another work group to describe their experience of a technique can be powerful.

Record Actions and Improvements

With parallel workgroups, a great deal of work can be undertaken. It is easy to lose track of what has been done. Careful recording of actions on an Action Plan is important. This provides an audit trail for what has been done, and a detailed accounting of actions that are still required.

It is tempting to delete things from the action plan as they are completed. It is more useful to archive what has been done so that reading the whole plan shows what has been achieved. This can avoid confusion in the group of what has been done, what is still to be done and what is out of the scope of the RPIW. It also supports the group by reminding them of all they have achieved.

Maintain Links between the Workgroups

Workgroups need careful management and support. Regular checking in with groups during work periods helps, as do regular meetings with the whole team. Joint meetings are important in keeping everyone up to date on progress, avoiding redundancy and keeping a sense of momentum. Where there are issues that cross workgroups, it is important that this is identified and that the participants speak to one another as required.

It is unusual for people to stay in the same workgroup for the entire RPIW. Tasks will often be completed, and the same group can be reallocated to a new task, or if it is appropriate, new groups can be created with people who were in different workgroups. A common occurrence is that there are a limited number of people with specific knowledge of a system, a process or a clinical issue. They may have to be moved between groups to allow them to benefit from the person's expertise. This can be frustrating for the individual as they may become interested in the work being done in a particular group. Explanation and negotiation can usually overcome this, for example, by having a person return to a group they are interested in after their contribution to another group. In other cases, their expertise is so important to the work that there may be no choice but to have them act as a technical advisor to several groups.

Make Use of the Advisory Group

The Advisory Group identified in the run-up to the RPIW can save much time and debate. They can offer advice on technical issues in their area and help to provide access to other teams or departments whose assistance is required. Assumptions made about the detail of a process outside the direct control of the team can cause problems, as it is easy to be wrong. Asking an expert can remove the need for much circular, and sometimes uninformed, debate.

Team members may also make assumptions about what a specific programme or technology can do or not do. It is common for teams to ask for a new piece of software to achieve a required action. When direct discussion with the relevant software experts is possible, it is often discovered that the existing software can do what is required but that the team was unaware of that function of the software. In other cases, an additional module exists that can do the required action but has not been purchased or has not been activated by the organisation, even when covered by its existing licence.

When dealing with software experts, it is useful to distinguish carefully between what can be done now, and what will require development so that the team are not over-optimistic. It is often better to develop a manual system and perfect it over weeks or months before commissioning any costly software changes.

Update and Expand Targets as Required

Some of the process targets may be achieved during the RPIW and this should be recorded. Other targets may be added or changed as evidence appears to challenge them. Additional balancing measures may be identified. These are often required to reassure the team that potential adverse impacts will be actively monitored. Some may be identified in advance of the RPIW, but others may emerge as the event progresses.

In the work of an RPIW, it is easy to get behind with administrative matters. This leaves a major burden for the facilitators and the Process Owner as the end of the event nears. Taking a few minutes every session to update any required changes pays dividends later in the event. Early in the RPIW get in the habit of updating the action plan regularly. As discussed in Box 10.1, 'Joint Working between Facilitators', facilitators can take turns to do this and, as the event progresses, support the Process Owner to update the plan. The Process Owner will take responsibility for the further development of the work after the RPIW, and it is important that they have a good understanding of both what has been completed and what remains to be done. It also gives the Process Owner an opportunity to demonstrate leadership to the team, and they can take responsibility for updating on progress if they have time.

Support Focus on the Aims of the RPIW

Mission creep is a risk. As the team delve into the details of processes, they often identify additional potential improvement work. If this does not relate directly to the aims of the RPIW, then it is important that it is identified, recorded and left aside. This can be difficult for team members to accept particularly if it relates to an area associated with their day-to-day tasks. The facilitators can help by making the list of recorded tasks in the parking lot visible, so that the participants know that an area important to them has not been forgotten. If necessary, the Process Owner can be involved in discussions so that the person is assured that they are aware of the potential for future improvement work on that topic. The Process Owner may be willing to commit to further review of the area.

Keep a Watchful Eye on the Team Dynamics, and Provide Support as Required

RPIWs often go very smoothly once people see evidence that they are being supported to improve their service and that their work will be directly beneficial to their clients. It is still useful to maintain a good overview of the team dynamics to minimise any problems. Issues that can arise include:

- **Overinvestment in one area of change.** If one area is going very well or is very important to some people, there is a temptation to pursue it at all costs. This can be the right thing to do, but it is important to balance undertaking more work than planned in an area against the progress of the whole RPIW. It may be better to move effort to areas that have not yet been pursued than to concentrate on a very few topics. Keeping sight of the aims of the RPIW and looking at progress across the Value Stream and across the breadth of targets can help when making prioritisation decisions.
- **Trying to induce a preferred change by force of argument rather than by testing the change.** Some ideas feel so obvious that their proponent may see them as 'just do it' issues. This is not the spirit of an RPIW. Any change is worth testing. Very rapid PDSA cycles can help to identify problems with an idea much more quickly than further debate, especially when some of the participants are certain of the outcome. Finding that an idea does not work

quite as anticipated is a powerful force for further change and testing.

■ **Some participants being marginalised in discussions.** As discussed earlier, organisational seniority should not be an important consideration in an RPIW. It can be sufficiently ingrained that it still affects participation. This can be by more senior staff feeling their views should be given greater weight, or by less senior staff being hesitant to offer their views and at times not feeling that they have a legitimate role in producing change. This is one of the most pernicious problems that can affect an RPIW, and it is essential to look out for it. Losing the views and ideas of the people who work closest with clients and processes, including patient and care participants, is an enormous loss and the facilitators and process owners must be alert for it. The response must be to support more junior staff to feel able to give their insights, and to support senior staff to hear those insights and to be prepared to act on them.

■ **User or carer representatives feel that their views are not being given sufficient attention.** This can be part of the issue above but can also arise when the person has had a very specific experience that has caused them great distress. Sometimes the process that caused the problem may have been removed, but the person still wants to address the problem in the previous process. At other times, it may be an issue which rarely arises. This does not mean it is not important to know about it, but it may mean that it cannot have undue focus despite its personal importance to the individual. In this situation, quantitative evidence that something seldom occurs is unlikely to have an effect: the person knows the harm it can cause even if it seldom occurs. The facilitators may need to support the person, and the group, to identify what can be done in the current process to minimise the risk of the adverse event or agree on how it can be looked at in more detail after the event. The explanation that improving the flow and reducing waste in large volume processes helps to free up time to deal with less common issues can be helpful in allowing people to move on with the main work of the RPIW.

■ **Staff, including advocates such as Trade Union representatives being very conservative about change.** Change often happens slowly in health and social care. One of the authors spoke to a staff member in a large healthcare organisation who was a member of a group tasked with revising one document, which had met monthly for over two years. This is extreme, but if people's experience is that change takes a long time, then very rapid changes

in a matter of hours can feel reckless and very risky. The assurance that all changes are being tested; that balancing measures are included wherever needed, and that all changes could be reversed if they do not work is usually sufficient. Trade Union representatives will want to protect and support their members but when they see that the people working in the service want to change the processes and that it is in the best interests of patients, they are usually satisfied. Understanding the nature of any remaining concerns helps to know how to respond so open discussion is best.

Work to Prepare the Process Owner for the Work Required after the RPIW

The Process Owner may be new to quality improvement and to Lean. They do not need to be topic experts, but they need to be confident that they can support the changes after the event and work with their team to make further improvements.

The facilitators should keep close links with the Process Owner throughout the event, as well as in the pre-workshop stage. Events can be challenging for the person in the Process Owner role. They are responsible for the service, and it is easy for them to feel that any problems identified and highlighted in the RPIW will be laid at their door. Even when they know they did not design the service they may feel blamed. The facilitators, and the Sponsor, need to make it clear that the work is about the process and that individuals are not being blamed for the previous process.

The facilitator also needs to have a good grasp of the Project Form and the Target Metric Report. They must understand how data was obtained and how the measurement can be repeated. Ensuring that the definitions of items and processes being measured and the way the data is obtained are clear can go a long way to reducing pressure on the Process Owner after the event. The Process Owner should also be supported to have a firm grasp of what is in the progress report and what still needs to be done. Time invested with the Process Owner during the event will help them after the event, increase their confidence and decrease the volume of support they require to carry the changes through.

Maintain the Housekeeping Tasks

These areas of the workshop need continuing attention. Availability of water, tea, coffee, etc., needs to be maintained. Areas need to be tidy and safe. Supplies of relevant documents must be accessible. Participants must adhere to any infection control requirements. When staff need to print out a form or a sign, the relevant equipment must be available. During an event, it is easy for housekeeping to get away from the facilitators, but it is important to keep on top of it. The wider group should be engaged with tidying, but the facilitators may need to prompt if required. Having the whole group engage in a brief organising session also helpfully demonstrates the power of regular team engagement in 5S.

Asking the group to record their satisfaction with the day using the same process as on Day One is useful to keep track of any emerging issues that may need to be resolved.

Ensure Involvement of the Wider Staff Group

The RPIW team undertake most of the work, but the role of the remaining staff in the service is very important. It is easy for the staff who are not part of the team to feel excluded. As the organisation conducts more RPIWs many more people will have an opportunity to take part, and this becomes less of a concern, but in early events, it is understandable if the staff not taking part feel that they are not part of the 'select' group and that other people have been chosen to make changes on their behalf.

There are several ways to tackle this. Briefings in advance, as discussed in the earlier chapters, and the opportunity to identify wastes and ideas for change are helpful. Treating the views of the wider staff with respect when trialling changes is essential. Staff are usually willing to try out a change and gain confidence when it is apparent that their feedback will influence the plan. Briefings to the wider staff group when any of the RPIW team are in the clinical or other area that is the subject of the RPIW are both courteous and helpful. On the final day of the RPIW, it can be good to deliver a Report Out on the work there, in addition to the lunchtime Report Out, as most staff will not have the opportunity to attend. The Process Owner can also work in the post-RPIW phase to promote ownership in the entire team by engaging all staff in further changes.

Make Use of the Sponsor

The Sponsor should return on the afternoon of Day Three as they did on Day Two. This is a further opportunity for them to shape the focus of the RPIW, and also to learn from the work of the RPIW team. Use the same process as described in Chapter 9.

The Sponsor can be brought in if help is needed with any problems, and they can aid links to other departments.

They can also help with prioritisation of resources and responding to requests over future commitments. It is usual to give participants in RPIWs' certificates of participation that they can use during their appraisals, and as evidence of the teaching in which they took part. Having these ready for the Wednesday afternoon Sponsor visit means that they can be signed in advance, ready for distribution after the Report Out on the final day of the RPIW.

BOX 10.1   PRACTICE TIP – JOINT WORKING BETWEEN FACILITATORS

The facilitators need to make active efforts to harmonise with one another. Some organisations have set roles for each facilitator during an RPIW, and this may be particularly useful in training phases. Once facilitators are experienced, it can work best if they allocate tasks between them as the event progresses. This does require openness and willingness to share work. Some facilitators may have preferences on what they do, but it is important that both facilitators feel that the work is equitably distributed. For example, if during one work period facilitator A supports teams and facilitator B updates documents, it is usually best to switch roles for the next period. Taking it in turns to lead feedback sessions is useful, and the Process Owner may want to take on this role over the course of the week. One facilitator may have experience with a specific task and find it easier, so there is no absolute rule on task allocation other than supporting one another to deliver the aims of the RPIW.

Preparing for the Final Day

As Day Four progresses, begin to sight the participants on the work of Day Five. Making it clear that there will be little scope to carry over any work to Day Five is valuable as it helps to manage expectations and to set a limit on the improvement work of the week. It is an opportunity to chat with participants about the parts of the work with which they feel most connection. This helps to give an idea of which part of the work the person may be comfortable presenting. It also provides a chance to speak to people about any anxiety they may feel over presenting.

Preparation for the Report Out is discussed in Chapter 11 as some facilitators prefer to do the work on Friday. Our experience is that a discussion between the facilitators and the Process Owner last thing on Day Four can help to smooth the work on Day Five.

Chapter 11

Day Five

Introduction

Reporting on the work is an important part of the process. This is often done in a session termed a 'Report Out'. The aims of the Report Out are:

- To describe the work and the solutions identified
- To celebrate the work of the team
- To share it back with the wider clinical team and other interested parties
- To reaffirm senior commitment to the work

In the timescale outlined in this book, the Report Out is delivered on Friday lunchtime after a weeklong improvement event. There is no hard and fast rule about this, but in a weeklong event, it works well to focus effort during the week and to give a clear endpoint to the Workshop element. Friday lunchtimes also work well because Friday is the end of the working week for some staff, and attendees often appreciate the opportunity to come together to meet one another and to catch up.

Preparing for the Report Out

The main principle is that everyone who takes part in the workshop should have the opportunity to report on the work. This is not always how things work in services. It is often the head of a team or working group who reports on the work with others looking on as they do so. In an RPIW, all the contributions are important, so it is also important that people's roles are recognised.

For some people, this will be an intimidating thought. If the RPIW has been successful in engaging a wide range of staff, the group will include people who often present at meetings or conferences and are very comfortable with

it but will also include people who rarely or never present and who may find the idea intimidating.

People sometimes want to say 'no' to taking part and make it clear that they would be happy to defer to others to present. Our experience is that people can almost always be supported to present at least something. No matter how worrying they find it, people are often exhilarated after the presentation. For some staff it will be the first time they have stood up at work, talked about some of their work and had all levels of staff including some of the most senior in the organisation listen to them. This has a very powerful message that the organisation is serious about valuing staff and that it recognises their contribution.

Preparing the Story

The workshop facilitators and the Process Owner can think about the final presentation as the week progresses. The main things to get across are the story of the work, the reason for it, the work done and what improvements have occurred or are expected to occur. RPIWs are rarely all that can be done, so also include what work is planned in the future.

It is easy to focus on the method and detail and to lose the overall narrative of the work. Considering how it relates to people who use the service and their experience of it can work well, as it helps to give an impression of the service user's journey.

Components to think about include:

What was the process that the team wanted to improve? Why was the work selected?

Consider showing the Project Form and pre-improvement metrics. Service user feedback before the event may also be relevant. A photograph of a waste wheel completed by the team in advance of the event can be useful.

DOI: 10.4324/9780429020742-11

What details of the process were identified during the preparation phase?

This will include any relevant details of observations. You do not have to describe everything, just enough for the audience to make sense of what was found. This may include examples of Direct Observation Records, Process Work Sheets and takt time calculations. Show the Value Stream Map as this gives a lot of information to people who are familiar with the format.

What targets were agreed?

Describe the targets set by the project sponsor.

Wastes and Ideas

Consider outlining how many types of wastes were identified in the process and how many ideas for improvements were produced. This helps to give an impression of the opportunities for improvement and the engagement of the wider team.

Future State

Briefly describe the ideas for a future state generated for the service. Showing a Process Diagram or other illustration of the proposed process is helpful.

Work Streams

Demonstrate the work streams undertaken:

- Describe the overall shape of the work – this will usually relate to the planned changes to the process.
- Have those involved in each work stream present the changes they made. This can be brief and there is not always time to include everything. Try to keep the story logical and understandable. Refer to the overall work stream diagram if required to reorient the audience.
- Showing what has been done can involve photographs, diagrams and forms showing new measurements and timings.

It is useful during the presentation to also link to the techniques that have been applied, such as error-proofing, as this helps the audience to see the linkages between the work and the method.

Changes Obtained

Show the revised Target Progress Report with any new timings. If these were measured in simulation, make that clear.

Show the revised Value Stream Map and briefly note the differences from the pre-event Value Stream Map.

Future Work

There are always more things to improve, so RPIWs are never the end of the story. Some things may still need to be done, new processes may have to be scaled up, and there may be other ideas identified in the RPIW which the team want to pursue. Giving an impression of the planned work is helpful to the audience and gives a base on which to build later Report Outs, as the action plan can be used as the base for updates.

BOX 11.1   SUMMARY OF SUGGESTED REPORT OUT ORDER

The general sequence is:

1. A description of why the work was prioritised – including the nature of the problems, and their importance and impact
2. What was found about the current delivery methods, including the opportunities for improvement?
3. How the work was structured – a description of the work streams that were conducted
4. Examples of the improvements that were trialled and agreed
5. The impact on the service, at least in simulations
6. The outstanding work to be completed over the next few weeks or months
7. Acknowledgements and thanks

Presentation Format

Avoiding overprocessing is an important Lean value. In presentations, particularly when senior staff up to and including the Chief Executive are expected to be in attendance, there is a natural desire to make the presentation look as professional as possible. This often leads staff to want to prepare a PowerPoint presentation. This, in turn, means that documents must be scanned, uploaded and incorporated into a presentation. It becomes far more difficult to then have rapid changes, and for individual participants to make changes.

The easiest way to avoid this is to use a visualiser. A visualiser is a device that allows a piece of paper to be shown directly. In the past, this was usually projected onto a screen, but now the input may go directly into a computer to be shown on a smart screen or similar device. Electronic visualisers are sometimes termed document cameras.

Very sophisticated versions designed for classroom or lecture hall use are available. These types may include other features such as high-magnification digital zooms and options to record. If these are useful for the organisation in other ways, then it may be sensible to buy a more capable device. For use in a Report Out, a basic machine with an acceptable resolution will do everything that is required. The main features to look for if buying one for Report Outs are plug-and-play USB or Bluetooth compatibility and that the device is sufficiently portable to allow it to be transported and used in different settings.

Process for Report Outs

Preparation: The Previous Evening

On the Friday morning, the time flies by. Getting work done the previous evening can make a huge difference to the smoothness of the session on the Friday, and to the stress of the participants. It is very useful for the facilitators and the Process Owner to spend some time on the Thursday talking through the story to share, although that is usually clear by that time.

When the team has left on the Thursday evening, the trio can prepare by pulling together the relevant documents, and getting things in the order they are likely to be used. This can include adding any summary sheets, or sheets summarising work streams. The group can also make a start on acknowledgements of people who have helped the team. Any other thanks that team members want to make, usually people who have helped with a workstream, can be added the following day.

It is also helpful to think about who would be best to present which part of the story. The facilitators can introduce the work and cover some of the background work. The Process Owner is likely to want to talk about the reasons for the work, and to pick up again later in the presentation to discuss what work still needs to be done.

Team members will talk about work in which they have been involved. People may have been involved in several work streams but to keep the presentation brisk it is best if each Team member only takes one presentation slot, unless there is a pressing reason to have them speak twice. The facilitators and Process Owner will know who worked on what, and how the story fits together. They can produce a rough storyboard to share the following morning. Having these things ready streamlines events the following morning.

Friday Morning Preparation

The Friday session needs to be brisk. There may be some issues remaining from Days Three and Four that Team members want to follow up, and this needs to be scheduled. Timing for the Report Out is important, particularly if other workshops are also reporting, or updates are to be presented from previous workshops. If possible, undertake the preparation session in the room in which the Report Out is to occur so that the group are familiar with the layout.

A rough sequence for the Friday morning session with a 9 am start is:

- Run through the thoughts of the facilitators and Process Owner for the Report Out. Check whether the Team members want to add anything or alter the emphasis.
- Give a provisional allocation of topics to people. Check if this feels right to the Team. Occasionally someone is more interested in talking about a different part of the work, and the arrangement needs to be re-jigged.
- Finalise the running order, and agree roughly how much time is available for each section of the presentation.
- Give people cards and ask them to prepare their comments. Ask them to be ready to run through the presentation by 10 am.
- Run through the presentation for the first time. Line people up in the same order as they are to present and encourage them to use the same presentation materials as they will use in the Report Out session.
- Time the whole presentation and the individual sections. Feedback on the timings to the group. The facilitators can also provide any qualitative feedback. This can include whether the mix of the material sounds right, whether it reflects the workshop adequately and any specific comments for individual presenters. Individual comments can be given at the time if appropriate, or if it feels more appropriate, during the coffee break.
- First attempts often run too long. Let people have a coffee break but agree on a time for the next run-through – 10.45 am is reasonable. During the coffee break and while people are preparing their revisions, the facilitators can circulate and check that people are content with their section and that they feel that it adequately reflects the work done.
- Have the second run-through, with the same process. Feedback as in the first session. This may be adequate, in which case staff can move on to agreement about post-RPIW tasks. If there are any issues with the presentation, there will be time for a third run-through if required.
- If the Report Out is happening in a different room, move the Team in plenty of time. Make sure that they are comfortable with any differences in layout, and any equipment differences.

Some people are very calm in rehearsal but become anxious as the presentation approaches. This may be more likely if the Team also must move room, and as the audience begins to arrive. The facilitators should keep an eye out for this and be prepared to offer support as required.

Evaluation questionnaires should be distributed to the participants to allow the organisation to obtain rapid feedback on the conduct of the event.

BOX 11.2   PRACTICE TIP – PRESENTATION

At the final run-through, collect the pieces of paper to be shown via the visualiser in the order the team bring them to present. Keep them together, in their correct orientation, and place them in a pile, in the sequence they will be presented, under the visualiser. One person, usually the Workshop Lead or the Team Lead, can then remove the pieces of paper as they are used, revealing the item below. This takes some practice but reduces the opportunity for the sequence to become muddled. It also helps to influence the pace of the presentation. In some cases, where multiple pieces of paper refer to the same work stream being discussed, the facilitator can remove the pieces of paper in rapid sequence, to give the audience an impression of the work that has been undertaken, without the presenter needing to dwell on the detail.

At the Presentation

The facilitators should check with the person chairing the session whether there is anything that the team need to know about, such as fire alarm tests. If there is no agreed process, the facilitators can also check how questions and comments will be managed and by whom.

Rather than have members of the team stand up and sit down, it is more straightforward to ask people to line up in order of presentation at the side of the room or side of the stage depending on the layout of the room. They can then come forwards in order, with the people who have spoken either returning to the end of the line or sitting down, if space permits. Seating arrangements can be made for any team member who is not able to stand for the time that would be required. Some team members, the facilitators and the Process Owner may be speaking more than once in which case they can re-join the line at the appropriate point. This sounds complex but after the run-through, participants are aware of the sequence and manage it well.

The session should start on time. The presentation should not be interrupted by questions, although there can be an opportunity for questions and discussion at the end. It can help if one person, usually a facilitator, remains near the projector after their section to ensure that there are no problems. They can help with any technical glitches and with moving paper on the projector if required (Box 11.2). It is fine for participants to read from cards if they prefer.

The Sponsor will want to feedback after the presentation and to put the work in a broader context. The Sponsor can also indicate what still needs to be done. The tone of the meeting is important. RPIW outputs are open to scrutiny, but the audience were not at the event and should not unduly second-guess the participants. Some organisations do not take questions at RPIW presentations for this reason.

There are often several possible solutions to a problem and that preferred by a senior member of the audience is not automatically preferable by dint of their more senior position. The session chair needs to manage challenges carefully. The facilitators can indicate the best person from the team to respond to a query or to provide clarification. It is common to find that most challenges have been considered during the RPIW. The discussion session needs to be brisk and if any individual point begins to extend to take up the time available, it can be moved out of the session if required with a guarantee of a later follow-up.

After the Session

It is good to have a short debrief and to check in with the participants. Usually, people have enjoyed themselves, sometimes despite earlier fears about presenting in front of an audience. A few people may feel they could have presented better, and it is important to reassure them if required. The Sponsor should speak to the group and thank them for their work. They can also present their certificate of participation.

As discussed in Day Four, it may be appropriate to run a separate presentation in the place of work for the wider clinical team. If needed, this does require organisation as it can be difficult to fit the required number of people into a space near a clinical area. If it is possible to continue to involve the whole RPIW team, it is best to do so as it gives the wider service team a good idea of who has been involved and the degree of effort and engagement.

The Process Owner and the Sponsor should make clear to the RPIW team what will happen next. Some changes may be ready to be implemented on the following Monday, other changes may require more testing or more preparation for introduction. Also address issues that were placed on the Parking Lot: the method for pursuing these should also be clear.

Chapter 12

After the RPIW

Introduction

The workshop is the most visible component of an RPIW, but the process includes the preparation phase and the follow-up. The follow-up can be one of the most challenging elements of an RPIW. The preparation phase generates interest and often some staff excitement, and the workshops are engaging and productive. There is often an upswell of pleasure and congratulation at the end of the workshop.

The day or week after the workshop the Process Owner returns to the workplace and must do their usual day-to-day job and implement, maintain and expand the changes identified. It is a truism that everyone has two jobs – to do their job and to improve their job – so some would argue that this situation is no different from usual. The changes that flow from an RPIW are usually substantial, however, and have happened very quickly, so there can be a lot of change management required. This means that the post-RPIW phase is important and merits thoughtful attention. A management system, such as daily management discussed in Chapter 13, can be helpful in sustaining the improvements and also in avoidance of duplication of effort. Metrics required for reporting are most useful when they are collected as part of running the business and not viewed as an additional burden.

There are three main trajectories that can emerge after an RPIW:

- Implementation of all the actions and changes, but no further changes
- Active engagement and continuous improvements in an energised team
- A gradual decline away from the RPIW improvements

The third trajectory is ruinously wasteful of the time, energy and hopes invested in the event. Maintenance of the improvements is the minimum that should be sought, but the best returns come from team engagement and the opportunity for the Process Owner and extended team to take the gains and the methods learnt in the RPIW and to extend the work to produce further improvements. The weeks following the RPIW are important in setting the course that is most likely to be followed. A management system, such as daily management discussed in Chapter 13, can be helpful in sustaining the improvements and in avoidance of duplication of effort. Metrics required for reporting should be collected as part of running the business and not created as an additional burden.

Meeting with the Process Owner

It is useful for the facilitators to meet with the Process Owner within a fortnight after the event. The Process Owner will have taken away the Action Plan and will now have had the opportunity to reflect on the event, the outcomes and the staff response. Immediately after the event, there is often a halo effect where the excitement and energy of the event carries the group along on a tide of optimism and hope for change. A few days or weeks after the RPIW, this fades and practical questions will begin to arise.

The Sponsor may arrange to be present but a session between the facilitators and the Process Owner can work well even in the absence of the organisational Sponsor. Understanding how the Process Owner feels about the RPIW process is important, and the debriefing also acts as feedback for the facilitators in addition to the questionnaire that was distributed to the RPIW Away Team on the final day of the event.

Issues to be discussed include:

- Engagement of the wider staff group
- Any issues identified since the RPIW

DOI: 10.4324/9780429020742-12

- The documentation and the information it contains
- Collecting new data
- The implementation plan
- Testing out further changes
- Preparing for update meetings

The members of the team who conducted the RPIW usually have a very good understanding of the event and its progress. Other staff members may be less aware and can sometimes feel excluded despite the best efforts of the facilitators and Process Owner to avoid this. Getting a feel for any evidence of this is helpful. If some people feel on the edge of the decision-making process, then the Process Owner taking the time to sit with them to explain the rationale for changes, and to emphasise the importance of team involvement, can be valuable. Ensuring that improvement work forms part of daily huddles is also important for team communication and involvement (see Chapter 13 for more discussion of Huddles and Daily Management).

Talking through any concerns about process changes that have emerged since the RPIW is a sensible step. It is always possible that a problem with one aspect of the RPIW-associated changes has emerged, and concerns should never be rejected out of hand. More often concerns arise because the reasons for changes have not all been apparent to people who did not have the opportunity to attend the whole week and the concerns can be resolved by discussion. If there is a newly identified problem, then rapid Plan-Do-Study-Act (PDSA) cycles to test out any required changes usually work well. It should not be assumed that the default is to return to a previous process given that the group decided that there was good reason to change it.

The facilitators can check back over the Project Form, the Target Progress Report and the Action Plan with the Process Owner. The Process Owner must be comfortable with the forms and more importantly the information they contain. The Process Owner should be encouraged to ask any questions or raise any issues about which they are unsure.

It is helpful to spend a portion of the meeting talking over the data contained and how progress will be monitored. Although the Process Owner will have attended all the Planning Meetings, it is often the facilitators who undertake the bulk of the data collection. The Process Owner must understand how the data was collected and precisely how each target is measured. They must be confident that they can collect the information and if they are not, the facilitators will need to offer additional support until this confidence is attained.

The implementation plan should be reviewed, and the order of further changes discussed. There are often actions left incomplete after an RPIW and going over the outstanding tasks helps the Process Owner. There may be some tasks that are more important than others, or actions

that logically must be completed before others. Working this through is valuable to the Process Owner.

The Process Owner will have a good idea of Lean methods and of how to conduct PDSA cycles from the Scoping Meeting, Planning Meeting and the RPIW. Beginning to conduct them alone may still feel like a big step. The facilitators can discuss what new ideas have emerged, and how they can be tested. There will often be unit quality improvement staff to whom the manager can be linked, and who can provide technical advice if the RPIW facilitators do not have the capacity to do so.

Update meetings can feel like an annoying obligation, distracting from what the Process Owner may see as their real work. This relates to the point above about incorporating data collection into the management process and making it helpful for day-to-day service management. If this happens, and the manager feels on top of progress with the Action Plan and ideas for testing out further improvements, the Report Outs become an opportunity to present ongoing work and to use data that is at their fingertips. The more the Process Owner can be supported to take this approach, the easier and more valuable they will find the follow-up period.

Update Reports

The organisation should not make update reports overly onerous. Their purpose is supportive rather than punitive. Their role is to:

- Act as a reminder that the RPIW is not the end of the work
- Share information on the work with the wider organisation
- Give the team an opportunity to celebrate their success
- Provide a problem-solving venue with senior staff if the team have encountered problems that they cannot resolve themselves

The frequency of meetings will vary by organisation, but three updates over six months to a year can work well. The reports do not need to be standalone meetings, and can be combined with feedback from new RPIWs, for example. If service users, carers or advocacy group representatives were involved in the original RPIW, it is good practice to invite them to the update session as they may otherwise not know what results came from their work.

At the minimum, the Project Form can be used to remind the meeting of the reason the work was carried out, of the targets and the main work of the RPIW. The Target Progress Report can be used to update on progress.

**BOX 12.1   PRACTICE TIP –
DEALING WITH PROBLEMS IN
THE RPIW FOLLOW-UP**

Data: If it is the first exposure of the Process Owner to Lean methods, they can take away the idea that measurement is intended only to check progress against the measures, and that checking the numbers the week before an update is due is fine. The data produced should be core to the process and should be part of the management information the Process Owner uses to run their service. Collecting information in real time and using it to make changes is both more likely to produce and maintain change and is also easier than a last-minute collection of data. Making the measurements part of the practice of the unit or service rather than an added burden helps the whole improvement process.

Change of personnel: If the Process Owner moves to a new post during the follow-up period, the staff member who takes the post may be at sea with the Lean methods and have limited insight into what prompted the RPIW and how changes emerged from the work. The Sponsor will have continued involvement and should be able to identify the personnel change. If this happens, then asking one or both RPIW facilitators to meet with the new staff member can be very valuable. Inviting the new staff member onto an RPIW on a different service can also give them an insight into what has happened and why.

Lack of engagement from managers: Sometimes the Process Owner is eager to keep up the work, but their immediate line manager has limited experience with Lean and of improvement workshops and offers limited support. This can be a considerable problem if the manager does not support the new Standard Work or take an interest in the changes and ongoing metrics. Staff attention is often directed by what is of interest to managers.

In this situation, the Sponsor may need to become involved. The Sponsor meeting with the line manager and explaining the organisational importance is powerful, particularly if they undertake to check in with the manager from time to time. This can change unwanted additional work into something in which the manager can take a pride, in which they understand the organisational importance, and which brings them into contact with and to the attention of senior staff. The Sponsor can also ask the relevant Director, if it is not themselves, to check in with the line manager to express their support for the work and to ask about its progress.

Other material can be added as required to illustrate relevant points, but numerical information on progress is essential.

The tone of these sessions is important. If they are seen as punitive, it will encourage staff to minimise problems and to emphasise gains. In the spirit of continuous improvement, it is vital to make it possible for people to talk about problems. Staff in the audience who trained in a Management by Objectives-oriented environment can sometimes use sessions like this to point score and to direct blame. It is very important that senior staff model the behaviour they expect: curiosity, encouragement and problem-solving are the order of the day, rather than blame and recrimination. These sessions can be large depending on how the organisation arranges the meetings: modelling behaviour for people that would lead them to see taking part in RPIWs as a route to criticism would be catastrophic for future engagement.

If the progress has not been what is expected, then understanding the problem and working out how to resolve it is what is wanted. In some cases, additional facilitator resource may be required to meet with the team to see what support is required. If a barrier in a different area has stopped progress, then the Sponsor should take a role in resolving any issues.

Conclusion

The post-RPIW work is part of the quality improvement effort. It should be conducted in the same spirit as the RPIW of engagement, respect and learning. Process Owners, particularly if they have been engaged in their first RPIW, will need support. An early meeting is very useful, and the Sponsor should ensure they engage with the Process Owner regularly.

The more that the work of the RPIW can be embedded in the routine work of the team, and the greater the extent that metrics are collected in the normal course of work and used for daily management, the greater the ease in maintaining progress. One of the outcomes of an RPIW can be to establish a group of staff who have experience in success with quality improvement and who are able to adopt the methods into their day-to-day practice. This can help to create model cells that people can visit when considering an RPIW or when they want to see a particular technique in use.

Every effort should be directed to making RPIWs both a success and a rewarding and enriching experience for a team. The more this is the case, the greater the pull of future improvement events and the higher the likelihood that teams will want to take part in improvement.

Chapter 13

Organisational Context

Introduction

Applying quality improvement methods such as RPIWs assists in solving complex challenges in organisations. In the context of health and social care, the results are often impressive (Burgess et al., 2022). Some organisations have been able to demonstrate considerable improvement in quality and reduction in costs. Others have had limited success, despite much effort. It is useful to explore why some organisations have been successful whilst others have not.

Quality improvement (QI) approaches can be applied at any level of an organisation. When looking for gains in the wider organisation, results are sometimes very local within one team or service, are confined to a few teams, or are short lived (Mead et al., 2023). This can be inefficient, costly and frustrating for those involved. It is important, therefore, to consider what elements constitute a positive culture of improvement to support front-line teams. Continuous improvement, kaizen events, small-scale initiatives and rapid improvement workshops all have a useful place. To maximise the gains from QI initiatives, it is important to consider how to create the conditions to embed continuous quality improvement throughout the organisation and to spread successful tests of change (Breckinridge et al., 2019).

Organisations which have been able to demonstrate sustained success have found ways to engage all employees continually and systematically in continuous improvement so that it becomes 'the way things are done here'. There is also strong senior leadership, visibility and regular reporting of initiatives (Lins et al., 2021).

A team or service can improve their own processes, and their patients will benefit from this. To produce successful QI at scale is a larger challenge and should not be the remit of a few individuals or even a quality improvement department alone: it needs to be the responsibility of everyone including the Chairman, Chief Executive and Senior Team, as well as all employees. To gain real traction, a quality approach should be the way business is done in the organisation and may require a radical cultural transformation.

Developing an organisational culture of improvement is neither easily nor quickly achieved. It requires strong leadership support, commitment and alignment. Successful organisations describe a 'journey' that has taken several years to embed and to be able to demonstrate tangible results. The learning from these organisations can help to accelerate improvements with the right approach, enthusiasm and commitment at all levels.

It should also be borne in mind when gaining organisational sign-up and attempting to describe the cost as well as quality benefits, that the improvements achieved may not always result in direct revenue savings. Although more difficult to quantify, the impact of cost avoidance, improved safety and harm reduction; productivity gains; increased efficiency through eliminating waste; improved throughput; patient, family and staff experience, including retention, must also be considered.

Attributing cause and effect in complex systems is challenging and some QI initiatives are shelved too early when cost reduction is not immediately evident, even if there are clear benefits for the service and patients. Improved outcomes for patients should always be the main aim of QI activity. That said, teams should not be put off if the rest of their organisation is not signed up for a wholesale QI approach. Any work that improves patient care and staff experience is still worth doing and small tests of change can be extremely powerful.

This chapter describes management approaches that can support RPIWs by helping to identify targets for improvement work and making it easier to sustain gains. When the whole organisation is not using an aligned management system, it is still possible to apply a Daily

Management System to support processes and to deliver improvements for patients.

Developing an Organisational Improvement Management System

World Class Management is a leadership system that provides focus, direction, alignment and a method of management of daily work. It comprises management by strategy for focus and direction; cross-functional management for alignment across the organisation for the benefit of customers; and daily management to ensure that teams and leaders have a system to help them know, run and improve their business (see Stark & Hookway, 2019, for a detailed discussion of management components in Lean; Figure 13.1).

Strategy Deployment

Ideally, there should be an organisation-wide approach to supporting the move from small initiatives or projects to an embedded culture of continuous improvement that strengthens the organisation. People require support and training to be able to identify and solve problems, improve performance and deliver value for their patients or customers (Hill & Canning, 2023). Rapid Process Improvement Workshops linked to organisational goals can contribute to this particularly when they have very senior sponsorship to assist with the removal of barriers and offer support for the maintenance of gains.

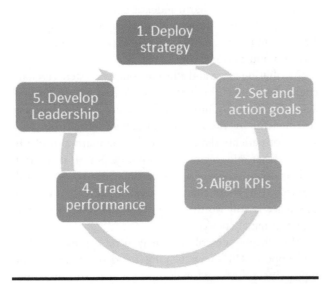

Figure 13.1 Components of a World-Class Management System. Adapted from Barnas and Adams (2014)

Developing a management system that connects the frontline to the Board Room/C Suite can go a long way to allowing this to happen. It can help to produce a system in which people speak the same language, understand the vision and direction of the organisation, and work together to achieve results.

Heath and care organisations often have a plethora of objectives and key result areas with staff feeling overwhelmed, confused and demotivated, harming performance. The key to success is to have a few 'breakthrough' objectives connected to the high-level vision (Colletti, 2013). This high-level vision is the 'True North' (Akao, 2004). This is the ideal state to work towards, and a small group of high-level metrics can be identified. This will help to produce organisational clarity on the direction of travel. This makes decision-making on priorities and investment easier at all levels of the organisation. Everyone should be able to relate to the high-level goals and identify their contribution towards realising them. This is alignment.

Alignment

Alignment includes clarity and openness on expectations. Some organisations develop a compact with employees to ensure that the expectations of all are agreed upon and aligned to the vision and core values of the organisation.

Often in organisations, improvement activity is scattergun, perhaps following the interests of the individual or group leading the work or by professional trainees who require to undertake projects as part of their course work. Individual projects are often excellent, but gains are not always maintained. Improvements may not be spread more widely and scaled up because the organisation is unaware of the work, often because the work is invisible to more senior staff who might otherwise be able to help with spread. In other cases, the work is not deemed to be sufficiently important or not an organisational priority. This may occur because of a lack of engagement of key individuals. Even very successful local initiatives may not be scaled up across the organisation.

It is important not to prevent local improvement work that is helpful to a particular group of patients, but alignment to the True North metrics assists in directing improvement work that is more likely to be supported, resourced, implemented, and rolled out. It assists by setting breakthrough objectives designed to make a difference quickly in a focused way as opposed to dozens of goals that cannot realistically be met.

Strategy Deployment is a different way of thinking about strategic planning and operationalisation. It may be worth considering using the same Lean methodology that we are learning about and carry out Plan-Do-Study-Act cycles to allow rapid testing and learning about the whole system.

Single Management Method/ System of Improvement

This book is about applying Lean methods to Rapid Process Improvement Workshops. A Lean management system can help the organisation to reap the greatest benefits from the work. Daily Management is a core component of any Lean management approach. This is aimed at continuous learning and developing people at all levels. It requires a shift in managerial mindset and behaviours from directing, telling and fixing, to enabling, coaching, mentoring and supporting. There are several components to a daily management system, and it works best when all elements are in place and working together.

This system relies on leader standard work throughout the organisation that reinforces, supports and improves performance at the frontline. The approach acknowledges that the staff and patients engaged in the day to day work are the experts on the processes they deliver and experience. The staff working in a service are the best placed to know, run and improve their business and to be accountable for delivery.

The actions and suggestions in the following section are intended to allow managers at all levels to reflect on how they can identify quality issues in their services, and how they can best support quality improvement. It can feel impossible to find the time to undertake QI work, and to support the changed work from an RPIW. Considering this section can help with that.

Components of Daily Management

Leader Standard Work

Leader Standard Work describes activities leaders should do daily, weekly or monthly to support the work of their teams. Using Leader Standard Work requires discipline and focus and should be aligned to organisational goals.

Leaders should take time to think about the core purpose of their role and to consider whether the activities they are undertaking are truly aligned to that purpose and to True North (Box 13.1). This is an essential part of achieving excellence by eliminating waste and reducing variation in the leader's work. It can help with prioritisation and in decision-making over what to get involved with and what to decline and can therefore be liberating. Leaders should model the behaviour necessary for an improvement culture and it is helpful when developing standard work to consider which behaviours will help in this. Status sheet

conversations are one example of what could be part of a leader's standard work.

BOX 13.1   ACTION – REVIEW OF ALLOCATION OF TIME

Using your diary and any notes, track how you currently use your time. What are the main categories of activity? Then calculate the percentage of time spent.

Areas of Work	%
Meetings	
Emails and other admin	
Writing reports	
Coaching/teaching	
Huddles	
RPIWs and other improvement work	
At the frontline	

Think about which activities you do daily, weekly, monthly or annually.

Honestly assess your current activity and consider what is adding value. Consider whether there are different ways of working that could reduce time spent at meetings or writing reports.

Consider what would you like to do more to benefit your people and your service. Identify the benefits of these actions and consider what behaviours you would need to display to work differently.

What conversations do you need to have to help you to implement your leader standard work? What have you learned by undertaking this review?

Status Reports/Sheets

Part of Leader Standard Work should be gaining a good understanding of the current state of processes and supporting staff to make improvements. Visiting the places where services are delivered provides opportunities to truly learn about the business, to help to identify patterns and issues and to find where best to focus improvement activities. This should happen every working day.

Status Sheets are a very helpful method by which to guide daily conversations between managers and staff during visits. Status sheets are also valuable in supporting leaders to learn how to ask open-ended questions on the gemba, the place where the work is happening. An example of a Status Sheet is shown in Figure 13.2.

Discussion areas		Notes
Safety		
Tell me about your patients at risk		
Have you had any recordable incidents in the past 24 hours?		
What quality issues have surfaced in the huddles?		
Tell me about your staffing and skill mix today		
Quality		
Discuss any opportunities for concern e.g. falls, sepsis		
What are you learning from your rounding?		
What processes are you monitoring today?		
Tell me about your improvement work, PDSA, any RPIWs?		
People		
Are there any barriers that I can help you with?		
Who needs most support today?		
Tell me about any additional staffing that you need?		
Tell me about any leadership issues		
Customer Service		
Any areas where demand exceeds capacity?		
How many patients?		
Has there been avoidable delay?		
What patient flow issues are you concerned about?		
What is your projected variance against targets? Is there a plan to manage the variance?		
What trends are you seeing?		
Cost		
Anything that will positively or negatively impact budgets?		
What did you do differently today to improve productivity?		
What is today's priority?		
How can I help?		

Figure 13.2   Example of a Status Sheet for a Manager

Use of a Status Sheet should be more of a conversation than a tick-box data gathering exercise. Leaders should adopt a humble inquiry approach and be genuinely curious rather than swooping in to 'fix' problems (Schein & Schein, 2021). There is no standard sheet that can be used in all circumstances. The sheet is developed by the leaders and a good Status Report will cover the key aspects that leaders need to know in order to be assured that the service is running as expected. It will also support them to coach and develop problem solvers at the frontline, to eliminate firefighting and to support teams. Questions should be aligned to True North metrics identified in the alignment process.

The Status Sheet is only a guide and follow-up questions can be added when necessary to help the leader to fully understand the situation and to be engaged in the conversation. Status Sheet visits are golden opportunities for early identification of trends that could lead to problems and for coaching teams in seeing those trends and taking steps to address the issues. Box 13.2 suggests developing a Status Sheet suited to the reader's service (Figure 13.2).

BOX 13.2   ACTION – DEVELOP A STATUS SHEET

Using the example in Figure 13.2, develop questions to fit your area of responsibility. Try it out and reflect on the value of doing this every day with the people who report directly to you. Consider what you would learn about your service.

A Status Sheet takes time to develop, and it can be difficult to know where to start. It can be useful to consider what worries about a service keep you awake at night. Consider what information would either reassure you or give you information on where improvement work may be required perfect and some people struggle with knowing where to start. Ask yourself, what keeps you awake at night and what information would reassure you or give you information to support improvement work.

Develop a few questions and try it out. Use a Plan-Do-Study-Act (PDSA) approach and learn as you practice.

If you use your new Status Sheet for a meeting, conduct the meeting close to the department QI or status board so that it can be used in discussions.

Huddles

Regular team meetings or 'huddles' are important in encouraging engagement of the whole team. They help to ensure good team communication, openness and transparency and encourage peer learning. They also help alignment of decisions at all levels with the True North organisational aims discussed earlier.

If Huddles are held regularly and use a standard format, they can save significant time and effort and avoid duplication of reporting. Huddles are conducted standing up. They are focused and very short.

The agenda is determined by the team performance and QI boards and covers the current state, lessons from the day before, horizon scanning, celebration and problem-solving.

Problem-solving should be conducted using PDSA cycles and agreed problem-solving tools such as A3s (Sobek & Smalley, 2008). Huddles require discipline and commitment and must happen at an agreed time, regardless of whether the leader is available. Any member of the team should be able to lead the huddle and senior leaders should be encouraged to attend to reduce the need for meetings and reports.

Making time for the huddle is not always easy and the team may require support from leaders to enable the protected time that they need. This might include an agreement on a later start to clinical activity; the creation of a 'no meeting zone' as part of the day, or a reminder that huddles are essential to the smooth running of the service and therefore should not be interrupted. Leaders may need to reinforce the importance of the Huddle with all staff groups including their leadership and managerial colleagues.

If the Huddle becomes the place to be to have issues aired and action taken quickly, if necessary, this will encourage attendance. As people see that huddling can reduce the number of longer meetings and emails, then they are more likely to be converted to this way of working.

Frontline improvement work can be identified by the teams and initiatives are then prioritised based on the organisational priorities. The teams, with leadership support, if necessary, are empowered and responsible for ensuring that improvement initiatives are integrated into daily work, implemented and sustained through regular measurement and reporting. Huddles are places where the need for RPIWs will be identified. When an RPIW has been conducted, the progress of the identified changes can then be reported daily at the Huddle to sustain the improvements.

BOX 13.3   PRACTICE TIP – HUDDLES

■ Agree on when the huddle is to happen. The team may need to play around with the starting time and length of the Huddle later, but just make a start.

■ Don't wait for all other elements to be in place: have a go, treat it as a small test of change and expect to make improvements.

■ Involve as many of the team members as possible. Ensure those that are unable to attend because they need to be with patients/clients can check the team board later for an update on what was discussed.

■ Encourage that wide attendance at every opportunity.

■ Working as a team, develop a Huddle Board relevant to your department/service.

■ Agree a process for the identification of possible improvement areas and at the huddle, Categorise them into improvements that can be done straight away; changes that require a PDSA cycle; problems that need more investigation of the root cause; and ideas that the team agrees not to progress.

■ Agree on who will do what and when they will report.

■ Think about performance – yesterday, today, anything we need to know about for tomorrow?

■ Celebrate!

■ Leaders should attend huddles regularly and use them as opportunities to learn, to support, to encourage and to remove any identified barriers.

■ Be committed and exercise discipline. Huddles should happen even when things feel chaotic, or personnel are missing.

Standard Work

Masaaki Imai said, 'There can be no improvements where there are no standards' (Imai, 1986, p. 74). Some people resist the idea of Standard Work, often because they fear that it will stifle creativity (Graban, 2014). When the root cause of a problem is understood and appropriate countermeasures have been developed, however, putting Standard Work in place to capture the best way of doing something as currently understood is very helpful.

Despite concerns about 'cookie cutter care', if the Standard Work is evidence based and has been developed and tested by the team involved, then it is more likely to be adopted and adhered to over time. Standardisation of best practice improves patient safety, drives out waste, reduces variation and is not person dependent. It helps with training and orientation of new and temporary staff, especially at busy times and can reduce costs. It is a crucial part of daily management.

Leaders should ensure that standard work is developed, implemented, maintained and reviewed. This is best done through direct observation, attendance at huddles and generally being present where the work is happening. When an improvement is identified, then the process can be revised using PDSA cycles and updated Standard Work created. Staff do not have to feel that it will be set in stone if further improvements are identified.

Problem-Solving

Leaders should encourage, train and coach front-line teams in problem-solving. This includes the use of tools to assist with systematic review of problems, root cause analysis and identification of possible solutions for testing. Quality improvement is a team sport. There is no need for highly technical tools, and many improvements can be identified, designed and tested using paper and pencil.

Teaching A3 thinking is a good approach. A3 refers to a sheet of A3-sized paper but the term is now used to refer to both a particular layout of a sheet and the thinking that underpins it. The sheet is used to describe the background to a piece of quality improvement work; the current state; analysis of the problem; small tests of change; and results. It is based on the Plan-Do-Study-Act cycle. A3s are useful for improving communication and developing a shared understanding of a problem as they are easy to display and share. They tell a story about the improvement work, highlight trends and successes and capture key details that can help understanding across the team. They are also a good vehicle to share work with other teams as once staff are familiar with them, they are straightforward to understand.

The key benefit is not the form, but the thinking that goes into an A3. Working with A3s is intended not only to support problem-solving, capturing and reporting activity, but also to help develop good problem-solving skills in front-line teams. Versions of A3 forms are available online and introductions to A3 thinking can be found in Shook (2008) and Sobek and Smalley (2008). Coaching people through thinking and testing are the most important aspects for leaders. A3s should be useful and not an additional burden.

If A3 forms are to be used, they must be maintained and updated to be effective. A3s are also an important part of visual management. As part of their standard work and status conversations, leaders can check that A3s are being timeously updated and maintained. This provides an opportunity for coaching conversations and for the manager and staff to reach the same understanding of a problem.

Visual Workplace

Being able to quickly check on the status of a service is an important part of daily management. This is where visual management is important. All too often notice boards are out of date and no one pays attention to them. Boards in a daily management system must be clear, easily understood and dynamic. Status Boards, Production Boards and Team Boards help with this. The following discussion focuses on clinical areas, but the same principles apply to non-clinical services.

A Status Board shows the state of the process and should cover the important aspects relevant to the team. It should be possible to understand the information on the Board within a few seconds while standing five feet away. The aspects of the process on the Status Board could include staffing, safety, quality, customer care and cost, for example. Progress can be coded red or green. This signals toleaders when they need to understand better what is going on and prompts the team to act. Status Boards are high-level summaries and will not normally contain any person-identifiable information, making it possible to locate them in patient areas where required.

Production Boards give more detail on the service and are used in the management of patients. They have person-identifiable information and are therefore located in staff-only areas. They can be whiteboards or electronic boards. Electronic boards will often be part of a patient management system, but in some cases are bespoke to the service area. There is often a progression from paper to whiteboard to electronic system as the team develops the information it needs to care for its patients. It is easier to make changes to a whiteboard than to an electronic system. Getting the information and layout right on paper or whiteboard versions can make the process of developing an electronic system much easier. Electronic systems need to be designed to support the process and taking the opportunity to be clear on what is required smooths the development process of a new electronic system.

The Team Board is a Board used to communicate with and between staff. It is very valuable in a hospital ward where there are several shifts, but it is helpful in any setting. It can include information on current quality improvement activities. This is important in encouraging team involvement, aiding communication and keeping track of ideas as well as highlighting topics for celebration.

These boards are where huddles should take place and they should provide the 'agenda' for the huddle. Senior leaders and colleagues should also be encouraged to view boards and attend Report Outs to aid sharing good ideas and the spread of successful tests of change. It is important that all leaders can understand boards and can have informed discussions with the team members.

Advisory Teams

Leaders cannot be experts in everything and should not be expected to lead improvement work on their own. Unidisciplinary management is not sustainable or advisable in integrated systems. Cross-functional leadership is a cornerstone of daily management. It helps people to move out of silos and to focus on value creation for their patients. It is important to find ways of ensuring that expert advice is available to leaders and teams involved in improvement work. An Advisory Team is a possible response to this.

An Advisory Team comprises multi-professional members who bring their knowledge from their area of expertise and are equal team members. Team members develop a sense of ownership for all the improvement work, not only their own area of expertise. Despite the term 'advisory', these team members are expected to contribute and engage rather than being passive or only offering advice. Advisory Team members should share the burden and be active participants, taking the lead on aspects of the work. Advisory Team membership can change depending on the needs of the service and the stage of improvement work.

Scorecard

In any area of work, it is important to measure progress. In daily management, key performance indicators are set, linking to the high-level goals and the True North metrics.

A Scorecard looks at the performance of key improvement initiatives. It requires a system for routine information updates to avoid having to look for data to feed reports. A Scorecard should have few enough measures to be easily understood with no more than five to eight targets. Scorecards should be cross-functional to demonstrate interdependencies and whole service performance. They are more formal than team boards or A3 reports and should be reviewed at least monthly. This forms part of leader standard work.

The senior leader's role is a commitment to the system and the teams. They offer support, encouragement, coaching and coordination. They should be visible and take responsibility for building quality improvement capacity and the expertise of staff. Leaders should also be sponsors for improvement events and free staff to participate in kaizen or Rapid Process Improvement Workshops.

Highly regulated environments can suppress creativity in finding solutions to complex problems. Trust, shared goals and relationships are required for success. Leaders must work to develop a positive improvement culture by creating a safe and supportive atmosphere that allows curiosity, experimentation and shared ownership of service quality.

Leadership

Supporting Quality Improvement in this way takes a new kind of leadership. Leaders must move away from blame, heroic problem-solving, control and old-style scrutiny to a management style which requires the skills of humble leadership, accepts that leaders do not have all the answers and actively involves people in finding solutions. Required skills include asking intelligent questions; helping to remove barriers; supporting quality improvement work; asking for input from others; developing staff; encouraging and rewarding progress and must be visible and approachable. This takes time. In order to free the time, non-value added activities, including some meetings, should be reviewed using the process in Box 13.1 and removed if they are adding no value. At an organisational level, a meeting free time slot can be agreed upon to allow leaders at all levels to be at the frontline.

Senior Leaders should be actively involved in improvement work. They are responsible for modelling the behaviours expected throughout the organisation. Leaders can participate in the development of the programme of improvement work; take part in some events; ensure that improvers have opportunities to report on their work and to seek to nurture the culture of continuous improvement.

For Rapid Process Improvement Workshops or Kaizen events, there should be a senior sponsor. Their role is discussed in detail earlier in the book. The leader should develop a good understanding of the tools and techniques and undertake training if possible. They need to attend the pre-event planning meetings and ensure that the necessary resources and permissions are in place. They can help to remove any barriers to the success of the event. For the event itself, the senior sponsor should be present at the start to set the scene, explain the links to organisational goals and strategy and to encourage the team. During the event, the sponsor will receive reports on progress and should be present at the final Report Out. Following the event, their responsibility is to ensure that the team has

the support and resources necessary to implement recommendations and should be visible on-site to encourage the team, to monitor progress and to ensure that findings are well reported and spread, thus avoiding unnecessary repetition and the sharing of learning. Box 13.4 summarises their responsibilities.

Ideally, the whole senior leadership team and the Board should receive regular reports from the teams themselves on improvement activity.

BOX 13.4   PRACTICE TIP – ACTIONS OF A LEADER IN AN RPIW OR KAIZEN EVENT

Be genuinely interested

Be involved in the discussion and decision about improvement priorities

Be present

Act as Process Owner or Sponsor

Attend planning meetings

Show up at improvement events

Be prepared to help to remove barriers to improvement, protect the team to allow them to focus and to negotiate with other departments, managers and if necessary senior leadership

Attend huddles

Conclusion

Improvement work is more sustainable and more effective if there is organisational support. Leaders have an important role in supporting quality improvement and in enabling improvement events. Individual leaders can provide support and encouragement in their own area.

At an organisational level, there is scope to introduce a Lean management system that aligns improvement priorities with organisational aims. This is a much larger-scale project. It is likely to bring greater gains, but it requires high-level commitment and steady endeavour over time. In organisations that do not use a Lean management system, it is still possible to use Lean improvement methods and to conduct RPIWs. In this situation, the leader and clinical team can use components of Daily Management to monitor the processes in the leader's area of work; to identify areas for improvement work; and to embed and maintain improvements.

BOX 13.5 REFERENCES AND SUGGESTED READING ON THE IMPLEMENTATION OF A MANAGEMENT SYSTEM

Akao, Y. (2004). *Hoshin Kanri: Policy deployment for successful TQM*. CRC Press.

Barnas, K., & Adams, E. (2014). *Beyond heroes: A lean management system for healthcare*. ThedaCare Center for Healthcare Value.

Breckenridge, J. P., Gray, N., Toma, M., Ashmore, S., Glassborow, R., Stark, C., & Renfrew, M. J. (2019). Motivating change: A grounded theory of how to achieve large-scale, sustained change, co-created with improvement organisations across the UK. *BMJ Open Quality, 8*(2), e000553. https://doi.org/10.1136/bmjoq-2018-000553

Burgess, N., Currie, G., Crump, B., & Dawson, A. (2022). *Leading change across a healthcare system: How to build improvement capability and foster a culture of continuous improvement, report of the evaluation of the NHS-VMI partnership*. Warwick Business School. https://warwick.ac.uk/fac/soc/wbs/research/vmi-nhs/reports/report_-_leading_change_across_a_healthcare_system_22.09.2022.pdf

Colletti, J. (2013). *Hoshin Kanri memory Jogger: Process, tools and methodology in successful strategic planning*. Goal/QPC.

Graban, M. (2014). Standardization is a countermeasure, never the goal. Lean Enterprise Institute [online]. https://www.lean.org/the-lean-post/articles/standardization-is-a-countermeasure-never-the-goal/

Hill, A., & Canning, G. (2023). Applying Kata in healthcare. In E. Mead, C. Stark, & M. Thompson (Eds.), *International examples of lean in healthcare: Case studies of best practices*. (pp. 165–182). Routledge.

Kenney, C. (2015). *A Leadership Journey in Healthcare: Virginia Mason's Story*. Productivity Press.

Imai, M. (1986). *Kaizen: The secret to Japan's competitive success*. Random House.

Lins, M. G., Zotes, L. P., & Caiado, R. (2021). Critical factors for lean and innovation in services: From a systematic review to an empirical investigation. *Total Quality Management & Business Excellence, 32*(5/6), 606–631. https://doi.org/10.1080/14783363.2019.1624518

Mead, E., Stark, C., & Thompson, M. (2023). Learning how to apply lean. In E. Mead, C. Stark, & M. Thompson (Eds.), *International examples of lean in healthcare: Case studies of best practices*. (pp. 207–217). Routledge.

Plesek, P. (2013). *Accelerating Healthcare Transformation with Lean and Innovation: The Virginia Mason Experience*. Productivity Press.

Schein, E. H., & Schein, P. A. (2021). *Humble inquiry, the humble art of asking instead of telling* (2nd ed.). Berrett-Koehler.

Stark, C., & Hookway, G. (2019). *Applying lean in health and social care services*. Routledge.

Shook, J. (2008). *Managing to Learn: Using the A3 Management Process to Solve Problems, Gain Agreement, Mentor and Lead*. Lean Enterprise Institute.

Sobek, D. K., & Smalley, A. (2008). *Understanding A3 Thinking: A Critical Component of Toyota's PDCA Management System*. Productivity Press.

Chapter 14

Conclusions

Introduction

Quality improvement is an essential consideration for all health and social care services. Lean is widely used in healthcare and has developed a considerable evidence base for effectiveness (Souza et al., 2021; Reponen et al., 2021). Lean focuses on delivering value to the people who use the service. With its attention to waste, flow and error-proofing, it has a natural fit with many of the preoccupations of the staff who deliver health and social care services.

Lean offers an approach to embedding QI in organisational work at scale (Mead et al., 2023). Marsilio et al. (2022, p. 3) describe Lean as 'organization-wide socio-technical performance improvement system'. This may be the ideal approach to gain the greatest benefits, but not all organisations are ready to move to an integrated Lean management system. Lean principles can also be applied at the Team and service level with considerable success (Graban, 2017).

This volume has described one way of applying Lean principles to tackle challenges in health and social care. Rapid Process Improvement Workshops (RPIWs) are a way of directing improvement efforts towards a problem in a way that can yield rapid benefits. It is valuable to consider how their effectiveness can be enhanced.

Key Issues in the Effectiveness of an RPIW

RPIWs are only one option for the application of Lean methods, but they can be very effective. Key considerations include the complexity of the problem and the ability of the organisation to devote the required time and resources for an RPIW. There must also be a commitment to follow up. As with any improvement work, it is easy to revert to the previous system and for gains to be lost. Effort after the RPIW is at least as important as the work undertaken before and during the RPIW.

Impact is enhanced when there is senior staff involvement. First- and second-line managers also have a big impact on the success of an RPIW. First-line managers usually see the benefits at first hand and senior managers will be sighted on the strategic benefits. Second-line managers are in the most difficult position. They are often not directly involved in an RPIW and are invariably juggling resources across a wider service. If they do not have a good understanding of the changes and why they were made, they are liable to revert back to previous ways of doing things when the resource is tight or demand increases. The book authors have seen several situations where an RPIW has identified flow as an important issue and has re-directed existing staff members to work on flow issues such as coordinating staff and materials and managing entry to and exit from a service. To a harried middle manager, it can look as if the staff member in this role is not contributing directly to the work of the team. The temptation to move the staff members back to face-to-face work with patients can be overwhelming. When this happens, the gains rapidly recede and are often lost completely.

Senior managers play an important role in this by encouraging middle managers to see the changes through. If the manager feels that they have a better idea, they can run Plan-Do-Study-Act (PDSA) cycles with the team to test it out. Reverting to a system that was already known not to work well without having anything better is rarely a good decision. System changes should be purposive and tested rather than rushed responses to stressors.

The Process Owner role has featured extensively in this volume. It is easy to underestimate the demands of the role as the person is doing three things – their usual job, the work of maintaining the improvements and ideally also leading the testing of further improvements. This creates substantial demands. Their immediate managers

DOI: 10.4324/9780429020742-14

have to value the improvement work or they will tend to ask only about day-to-day demands which tend to refocus the Process Owner on business as usual. Creating Leader Standard Work for both the Process Owner and their manager can help to alleviate this pressure and help the Process Owner to feel supported and valued.

Team members can find the contrast between the openness and pressure for change in an RPIW and the difficulty in making improvements at other times dispiriting. Returning to previous ways of doing things where they find it difficult to communicate their ideas with any expectation of change can be very disappointing for staff who have felt empowered and heard during the work of an improvement event. Our experience is that the best way of dealing with this is to make daily work more like the best aspects of an RPIW. This demands respect for staff and mindful attention directed to their observations and ideas for change. Allowing open discussion of service problems and encouraging identification and testing of ideas maintain momentum and help to provide team ownership of problems and solutions. The methods described in Chapter 13 of using Huddles and Team Boards to support this change work well.

In an analysis of the impact of five English NHS Trusts partnering with the Virginia Mason Institute and applying Lean methods, all five showed a decreased trend in the number of staff leaving the Trust (Burgess et al., 2022). Staff are the chief resource of any care delivery organisation, and recruitment and retention are a challenge because of competition from other employment sectors and even other countries. Increasing enjoyment at work and helping staff to feel in control of their work and able to make improvements can help to make an organisation a better employer.

Staff who have taken part in improvement work can also act as advocates within the wider health and social care system. As noted earlier, testimonies to effectiveness from staff are likely to be far more persuasive than any number of corporate communications. Burgess et al. (2022) in a survey of staff in the English healthcare systems receiving support from the Virginia Mason Institute, 96% of respondents supported the use of Lean in healthcare and 84% valued the effect of Lean on their work. The main barriers to the application of Lean were reported as time (66%) and the pressure to meet targets (35%).

These barriers are likely to exist in all health and social care settings. RPIWs are an effective way of creating dedicated time for improvement work, but for the events to have their maximum potential it is necessary to make it possible to engage in day-to-day quality improvement work all year-round. An RPIW provides a good opportunity to take stock of the whole system in the relevant clinical area and to consider how to maximise staff

opportunities for improvement work. It is also a good time to reflect on the potential role of daily management and to make any required changes to the management system. Showing staff that quality improvement is an ongoing focus for the organisation and not only something that is conducted in response to a problem can help to secure the staff investment that is essential for continuing gains.

Measurement is a fundamental part of quality improvement work. Used well, it both supports change and identifies opportunities for further improvement (Graban, 2019). Staff in clinical areas and in support services often have very little access to performance and financial information. Good data, available quickly, is an ideal support for quality improvement activity (Cordiner et al., 2023). In the follow-up to an RPIW, it is vital to review the relevant metrics. As discussed in Chapters 12 and 13, this should not be an afterthought with data gathered only to allow an update to an RPIW at a Report Out. The data has to be part of the Daily Management system, allowing staff to know how their process is performing and allowing them to take action to investigate and if necessary amend their processes if the information shows problems.

Conclusions

Rapid Process Improvement Workshops are an effective tool that can spark long-term change that can be transformational for a team and its service. The precise approach will vary by organisation, but this book sets out a process for their application in health and social care settings. Our experience is that RPIWs repay the effort and application that is invested in them. When the facilitators, the Process Owner, Sponsor and team members all engage in the process, the returns can be substantial.

Finding the time for RPIWs and other improvement work can seem impossible for a hard-pressed organisation, but the existing situation is a result of the processes that have built up over time and of the work requirements for the service. Although it may not be possible to amend the demand for the service it is certainly practical to review and revise the processes that the service uses.

Change is difficult and can be threatening. Putting staff and service users at the heart of improvement activity and focusing on the needs of patients helps to give a direction to improvement work that is acceptable to all staff groups. Cost savings often result from better control of processes but even when there are no cost savings, benefits can include decreased waits, decreased errors and increased quality. The best ways of dealing with staff concerns are openness and systematic efforts to engage staff in quality improvement work. Respect is a fundamental tenet of the Lean approach, and it is imperative that it is demonstrated throughout the change process.

Lean methods began in industrial settings but many service and care organisations have found the methods applicable and beneficial. There is evidence from across the world that Lean approaches can have positive effects in health and social care settings in very different care delivery systems (Mead et al. 2023). The methods described in this book will support change, staff engagement and quality improvement. RPIWs are not always the right tool for the job, but when they are conducted, the best results come from attention, systematic application of method and consistency over time.

References

Burgess, N., Currie, G., Crump, B., & Dawson, A. (2022). *Leading change across a healthcare system: How to build improvement capability and foster a culture of continuous improvement, report of the evaluation of the NHS-VMI partnership.* Warwick Business School. https://warwick.ac.uk/fac/soc/wbs/research/vmi-nhs/reports/report_-_leading_change_across_a_healthcare_system_22.09.2022.pdf

Cordiner, K., Gupta, P., Arafa, S., Stark, C. (2023). Value management. In E. Mead, C. Stark, & M. Thomson (Eds.), *International examples of lean in healthcare.* (pp. 59–75). Productivity Press.

Graban, M. (2017). *Lean hospitals: Improving quality, patient safety, and employee engagement* (3rd ed.). CRC Press.

Graban, M. (2019). *Measures of success: React less, lead better, improve more.* Constancy, Inc.

Marsilio, M., Pisarra, M., Rubio, K., & Shortell, S. (2022). Lean adoption, implementation, and outcomes in public hospitals: Benchmarking the US and Italy health systems. *BMC Health Services Research, 22*(1), 1–10. https://doi.org/10.1186/s12913-022-07473-w

Mead, E., Stark, C., & Thomson, M. (2023). Learning how to apply lean. In E. Mead, C. Stark, & M. Thomson (Eds.), *International examples of lean in healthcare.* (pp. 207–217). Productivity Press.

Reponen, E., Rundallo, T. G., Shortell, S. M., Blodgett, J. C., Juarez, A., Jokela, R., Makijarvi, M., & Torkki, P. (2021). Benchmarking outcomes on multiple contextual levels in lean healthcare: A systematic review, development of a conceptual framework, and a research agenda. *BMC Health Services Research, 21*(1), 1–18. https://doi.org/10.1186/s12913-021-06160-6

Souza, D. L., Korzenowski, A. L., Alvarado, M. M., Sperafico, J. H., Ackermann, A. E. F., Mareth, T., & Scavarda, A. J. (2021). A systematic review on lean applications in emergency departments. *Healthcare, 9*(6), 763. https://www.mdpi.com/2227-9032/9/6/763

Index